God's New Whiz Kids?

God's New Whiz Kids?

Korean American Evangelicals on Campus

Rebecca Y. Kim

NEW YORK UNIVERSITY PRESS
New York and London

NEW YORK UNIVERSITY PRESS
New York and London
www.nyupress.org

Library of Congress Cataloging-in-Publication Data
Kim, Rebecca Y., 1957–
God's new whiz kids? : Korean American evangelicals on campus /
Rebecca Y. Kim.
p.   cm.
Includes bibliographical references and index.
ISBN-13: 978-0-8147-4790-2 (cloth : alk. paper)
ISBN-10: 0-8147-4790-6 (cloth : alk. paper)
1. Church work with Korean Americans. 2. Church work with
students. 3. Evangelistic work. 4. College students—Religious life.
I. Title.
BV4468.2.K6K56 2006
277.3'083089957—dc22   2006016112

New York University Press books are printed on acid-free paper,
and their binding materials are chosen for strength and durability.

Manufactured in the United States of America
10 9 8 7 6 5 4 3 2 1

To My Parents

Contents

Acknowledgments

There are many people to thank. I am grateful to the various unnamed students, pastors, staff, and administrators who welcomed me into their fellowships and made my research possible. I thank my mentors Min Zhou, Roger Waldinger, and John Evans, as well as various scholars including Russell Jeung, Antony Alumkal, Pyong Gap Min, and Stephen Warner, whose works have shaped my thoughts and writings on the second generation. The support of various organizations and institutions including the Louisville Institute, the Society for the Scientific Study of Religion, the LeRoy Neiman Center for the Study of American Society and Culture (UCLA), and the Institute for American Culture and the Asian American Studies (UCLA) have also been invaluable. Finally, I express much thanks to my dear parents, husband, and friends for their continued love, encouragement, and faith.

Introduction

> At lunchtime, one need only walk into Berkeley's Sproul Plaza, that famed arena of leftist politics, to note the transformation: where a salvo of free speech and anti-war slogans could once be heard, mantras of religious recruitment now drown out all sounds of protest. Pamphlets promising salvation, karaoke and full immersion baptism, all in the same night, are proffered eagerly by members of the Evangelical Formosan Church, the Asian American Christian Fellowship and the Chinese Graduate Christian Society.
> —Carrie Chang, *Amen. Pass the Kimchee,* 2000

Whether studying the Bible at Berkeley, engaging in feverish prayer at Harvard, or singing "praise" at Yale, Asian American Christian fellowships have become a familiar sight at many of the top colleges and universities across the country. Today, there are more than fifty Evangelical Christian groups at the University of California (UC) at Berkeley and the University of California at Los Angeles (UCLA), and 80 percent of their members are Asian American (Busto 1996; Chang 2000; Hong 2000). On the East Coast, one out of four Evangelical college students at New York City colleges and universities are Asian American (Carnes and Yang 2004).[1]

At Harvard, Asian Americans constitute 70 percent of the Harvard Radcliffe Christian Fellowship, and, given the popularity of Evangelical Christian fellowships, one can easily spot students who proudly don T-shirts with phrases like "the Asian Awakening" (Chang 2000: 1). At Yale, the Campus Crusade for Christ is now 90 percent Asian, which is astonishing considering that twenty years ago it was 100 percent white. Like Yale, Stanford's InterVarsity Christian Fellowship (IVCF) has become almost entirely Asian (Chang 2000). Moreover, the growth in the number of Asian American Evangelicals is obvious at other IVCF chapters in the nation.

With about 650 chapters at universities across America, IVCF saw the number of Asian Americans grow by 267 percent nationwide over the last 15 years, from 992 to 3,640. In New York and New Jersey, the number of Asian Americans increased by 605 percent, from 97 to 684.[2] Not surprisingly, the percentage of Asian Americans at InterVarsity chapters on some West Coast and Northeast campuses and throughout parts of the Midwest is often as high as 80 percent. Up until the 1990s, IVCF's triennial missions convention, Urbana, was predominately white. In 2000, however, it was 26 percent Asian American (Tokunaga 2003: 167). The ten largest InterVarsity chapters with a high percentage of Asian Americans include Cornell, Northwestern, Rutgers, University of Illinois–Chicago, Boston University, University of Michigan, Emory, University of Washington, Harvard, and the Massachusetts Institute of Technology.

Among the growing Asian American campus fellowships, second-generation Korean American (hereafter, SGKA) fellowships are the most visible, particularly on the West and East Coasts. For example, UCLA alone boasts of more than ten Korean American Christian fellowships. The growth of Korean American campus fellowships, however, is not restricted to the coasts; virtually every top-ranking university and college across the country has at least one Korean American campus fellowship. SGKA Evangelicals and their Christian fellowships not only embody but also constitute a major part of the surge of Asian American Evangelicals on elite campuses in the United States.

This book investigates this newly emerging phenomenon. Focusing on SGKA Evangelicals, it looks at the growing numbers of Asian American Evangelicals and their ethnic campus ministries. Specifically, it examines why Americanized SGKA Evangelicals from middle-class, largely white, suburban neighborhoods on a campus with a host of ethnically diverse religious organizations are flocking to separate ethnic campus ministries. The book explores this paradox: ethnic religious organizations have shed most of the practices and rituals of their ethnic community and embrace dominant, white Evangelical practices and rituals, yet they resist assimilation and maintain ethnic segregation.

Asian American College Evangelicals

The majority of Asian American college Evangelicals are U.S.-born Korean Americans and Chinese Americans, both of whom largely come from middle-class families, grew up in white or racially mixed suburbs, and are familiar with mainstream culture and organizations. They have few barriers in participating in mainstream Christian organizations and can be considered "successful" in terms of their educational and future occupational status. Asian Americans' median household income in 1999, $55,525, was the highest of all racial groups (including whites), and their poverty rate, 10.7 percent, was the lowest of all racial groups; 44 percent of Asian Americans over the age of 25 had a least a bachelor's degree—18 percentage points more than all other racial groups (Zhou 2004). Asian Americans account for only 4 percent of the U.S. population, but they account for more than 6 percent of college enrollment nationwide, and at the Ivy League universities Asian American enrollment often exceeds 20 percent (Hong 2000; Zhou and Gatewood 2000). Likewise enrollment of Asian Americans in California's public universities is disproportionate to their 10.9 percent of the state's population (U.S. Census, 2000). Asian Americans currently make up over 40 percent of the student population at UC Berkeley as well as UCLA and 50 percent of the student population at UC Irvine (Zhou and Gatewood 2000).[3]

By the second generation, most Asian Americans lose fluency in their parents' native language and speak only English. Asian Americans also intermarry extensively with whites, and more than 25 percent of Asian Americans have a partner of a different racial background (Lee and Bean 2003, 2004). Furthermore, leaders in the Evangelical Christian community have eagerly labeled Asian Americans as the moral model minority, as "God's new whiz kids"—who excel not only in school, but in faith (Busto 1996): "Not only are they smart, hardworking, and graduating from prestigious universities, but they are godly as well!" (Jeung 2005: 5). They have become the icons of active, if not aggressive, campus Evangelicals—to which other Evangelicals should aspire.

Despite their socioeconomic status, acculturation, and entrée into mainstream institutions, SGKA and other Asian American Evangelicals are flocking to separate ethnic campus ministries over multiethnic or predominately white Evangelical organizations. This pattern conflicts with assimilation theories that expect ethnic identification to decline, not increase, with socioeconomic mobility and entrance into mainstream institutions and organizations (Alba and Nee 1996; Gans 1992; Gordon 1964; Park 1950). Why would young Asian American adults who have grown up in white or racially mixed communities choose to affiliate themselves with ethnically separate ministries on campus?

Assimilation and Pluralist Theories

The classic assimilation model predicts that immigrants will integrate into mainstream society in a smooth, irreversible, linear, and inevitable fashion (Park 1950; Warner and Srole 1945). Ethnicity is viewed largely as a working-class phenomenon—something that immigrants and their descendants need and want to shed as they acculturate, obtain economic mobility, and incorporate into the dominant society. As immigrant ethnic groups shed their ethnicity, the dominant group, defined commonly as the white Anglo-Saxon Protestant middle-class, is expected to undergo little or no change.

Having been formulated to explain the experiences of European immigrants at the turn of the twentieth century, classic assimilation theory has been criticized for being unable to describe the experiences of contemporary post-1965 immigrants. Compared to the past European immigrants, today's immigrants are far more racially diverse and face an hourglass economy that offers relatively little opportunities for immigrant children to gradually achieve economic mobility (Portes and Zhou 1993). Assimilation theory has also been criticized for its ethnocentric Anglo-conformist bias. Among the problems with the theory are that it focuses only on the relationship between the immigrant and dominant group and ignores the relationships among minority groups that may affect the assimilation process (Brubaker 2001); does not consider how the majority group may change in the process of assimilation (Alba and Nee 2003); assumes that immigrants have little agency and choice in the process of assimilation; implies that it is in the minority's best interest to assimilate (Gibson 1988; Portes and Bach 1985; Yang 1999); and offers an unrealistic homogenous view of U.S. society.

One of the popular reformulations of assimilation theory that has responded to these criticisms is Portes and Zhou's (1993) segmented assimilation theory. Depending on immigrants' pre-migration characteristics, particular forms of exit and reception, size, structure, and resources of existing co-ethnic communities, location and economic and political context of settlement, and expectations of immigrant children, Portes and Zhou propose three paths of assimilation. First, some will follow the traditional path of incorporation and assimilate into the white middle class. Second, children of immigrants who lack strong ethnic communities and mobility ladders, and who are concentrated in an urban city with a hostile minority subculture, may permanently assimilate into a minority underclass. Third, those who have the support of strong and resourceful ethnic communities can circumvent outside hostility and mobility obstacles to achieve economic advancement while maintaining ethnic ties and preserving immigrant community values.

Segmented assimilation theory skillfully accounts for the diversity of today's immigrants and the cultural and structural pluralism in U.S. society without abandoning the concept of assimilation. It no doubt improves upon the classic assimilation model, but the theory likewise has its limitations.

Because segmented assimilation theory focuses mostly on the structural assimilation of the children of contemporary immigrants (their educational and occupational mobility), what happens to their ethnic identities after structural assimilation is not addressed. Segmented assimilation theory assumes that those who have difficulty attaining socioeconomic mobility and are in danger of assimilating into a minority underclass may turn to ethnic communities for support and increase their ethnic affiliation. But it has difficulty explaining why and how those who are already middle class and are not dependant on the ethnic community for mobility would symbolically and practically maintain strong ethnic ties. Related to this, segmented assimilation theory does not explain exactly what individuals are assimilating into, aside from the white middle class or the minority underclass. For example, some of today's children of immigrants are expected to achieve rapid economic advancement by deliberately preserving elements of the immigrant community's values and maintaining strong ethnic ties. But what happens to these children after they have obtained structural mobility? Will they become "like" the white majority, will they continue to maintain separate ethnic boundaries, or will something else happen to them? What does it mean for the children of today's immigrants to "assimilate" when they have already obtained educational and occupational mobility? The answer is not clear.

Multicultural and pluralist theories do not have a problem explaining the resilience of ethnicity. American society is assumed to be heterogeneous, and ethnicity is argued to remain significant for multiple reasons. First, it persists because of rational interests. Ethnic groups are defined essentially as rational interest groups who struggle to gain benefits in an unequal competitive society through organizing around ethnicity. Individuals form ethnic groups because of the "strategic efficacy of ethnicity in making legitimate claims on the resources of the modern state" (Glazer and Moynihan 1975: 11)—because it helps them to advance their economic and political interests. Thus, ethnicity lives on because it can become a means of claiming advantage in a competitive society (Bell 1975; Calderon 1992; Lopez and Espiritu 1990; Nagel 1986; Okamoto 2003).

Others criticize this conceptualization of ethnicity as simply a means to maximize group interests and argue that ethnicity is qualitatively substantial and made up of the cultures and heritages passed on from past generations. The persistence of cultural heritage is the basis for the continued importance placed on ascriptive groups (Abramson 1973; Greeley 1974). The problem with cultural heritage theories of ethnicity, however, is that it is not clear how ethnicity gets transmitted to the next generation and what exactly is retained by the later- generations who do not have any direct ties to the home country.

In contrast to cultural theories of ethnicity, symbolic ethnicity theory proposes that ethnicity exists only in insignificant symbolic forms. Herbert Gans (1979) contends that among third- and fourth-generation European Americans there is a new form of "symbolic" ethnicity, an ethnicity that is concerned more with the sociopsychological elements of "feeling" ethnic rather than actually being part of an ethnic culture and community. Ethnic symbols are consumed and used to identify with a particular ethnicity without being socially tied to a particular ethnic group. Thus, if ethnicity exists at all, it becomes largely expressive and symbolic—something of a "leisure-time activity." This kind of optional symbolic ethnicity, however, is not a reality for later generations of Asian Americans who are continuously racialized and treated as physically distinct (Jeung 2005; Kibria 2002; Min 2000; Tuan 1998).

According to William Yancey et al. (1976), ethnicity is not merely symbolic, a product of competing interest groups, nor is it made up of inherited cultures. Instead, it is "emergent" and continuously constructed under the structural conditions that characterize urban American life. Criticizing both assimilation and pluralist theories, Yancey and his colleagues argue that ethnicity emerges and develops because of the social structural constraints of occupation, residence, and institutional affiliations. Ethnicity, as defined by identification with common origins and frequent patterns of association (Greeley 1974; Haller 1973), is "generated and becomes crystallized under conditions of residential stability and segregation, common occupational positions and dependence on local institutions and services" (Yancey et al. 1976: 399). Thus, ethnic identification and association persist and take shape within the structural parameters that characterize urban working-class life.

Most contemporary immigration scholars (even assimilationists) would not dispute the claim that ethnicity is emergent and reconstructed in America. Many would agree that ethnicity continues to change and unfold and is not a constant ascribed trait inherited from a foreign land (Conzen et al. 1992; Rumbaut and Portes 2001). They would also agree that ethnic identification and association can be strong in ethnic urban settings. But the issue is whether this kind of emergent ethnicity can be constructed beyond the kind of urban ethnic community that Yancey et al. (1976) describe. In other words, why and how does ethnicity remain significant for later generations, who are more mobile and acculturated and are not residentially and occupationally segregated and dependent on local ethnic institutions for survival? Like the assimilationist approach that they criticize, Yancey et al. (1976) cannot explain this. Ethnicity is still viewed as a working-class phenomenon—the "stuff" that comes out of urban ethnic ghettos.

Moreover, Yancey et al. (1976) do not explain what draws individuals to form ethnic group boundaries at the microgroup level. They reject cultural heritages as the basis of ethnic groupness and argue, instead, that structural conditions are paramount. Having rejected cultural arguments, however, they do not offer any alternative explanation as to why individuals identify and associate ethnically when given the structural opportunities to do so.

Relatedly, Yancey et al. (1976), like the pluralists that they criticize (Abramson 1973; Greeley 1974), do not explain how ethnicity changes and what gets retained over generations. Yancey et al. (1976), along with many others (e.g., Conzen et al. 1992), argue that ethnicity is constructed in the urban ethnic communities of America, that the "so-called foreign heritage" takes shape in America. But they do little to address how ethnicity then changes for the later generations; they do not explain what may or may not be retained from the urban ethnic communities of America to make ethnicity salient for later generations. If second and later generations are maintaining strong ethnic group boundaries, what is the substance of those boundaries? How do they differ from those of the first generation and those in the larger mainstream society?

Second-Generation Asian Americans' Religious Participation

Studies on second-generation Asian Americans' religious participation remain relatively scarce. But there is an emerging literature on the topic that explains why Asian Americans, including SGKAs, would participate in separate ethnic religious organizations. The literature points to racialization and ethnicization explanations.

According to racialization perspectives, different Asian ethnic groups develop solidarity based on their dawning recognition that they are treated by others as distinct primarily because of their physical appearance (Alumkal 2002; Emerson and Smith 2000; Jeung 2000, 2002). Racialization theories stress experiences of marginalization and being marked as different, particularly by the majority or hegemonic group(s), as the basis of ethnic or pan-ethnic grouping.

For example, Antony Alumkal (2002) argues that Asian Americans turn to Evangelical campus fellowships as an act of self preservation in a racially hostile setting. Rudy V. Busto (1996) similarly argues that Asian Americans "retreat into Evangelicalism" on the "increasingly racialized college campus where Asian American students are imaged as competitive, overrepresented and culturally monolithic" (37). Examining the reorganization of Chinese and Japanese American congregations around a new pan-ethnic Asian American identity, Russell Jeung (2000) adds that contemporary Evangelicalism gives Asian Americans a chance to escape the undesirable aspects of their racial status by making Christianity the locus of their identity; that is, ethnic or racial distinctions are transcended through a relationship with God. Racialization perspectives thus suggest that Asian Americans turn to Evangelical fellowships, including pan-ethnic Evangelical fellowships, to escape a society where "race" continues to matter.[4]

By making "race" the operative principle of social differentiation, racialization theorists suggest that SGKAs would be equally comfortable in pan-Asian congregations where their fellow members are Chinese and Japanese Americans. This, however, is not the case. Few SGKAs participate in pan-ethnic Asian American campus ministries when given the choice to participate in separate ethnic campus ministries of their own. Furthermore, most of the large Asian American campus Evangelical organizations (including Asian American churches) tend to be predominately Chinese or Korean American; pan-ethnic ministries with a sizable mix of the different Asian ethnic groups are scarce.

By contrast, while acknowledging the significance of racial ascription and adversity, ethnicization perspectives stress cultural distinctiveness as the primary source of continuing ethnic religious group boundaries. According to the ethnicization perspectives, individuals cluster together in separate ethnic groups because they share common cultural experiences that make them distinct from others (Chai 1998; Chong 1998; Goette 1993; Smith 1978; Warner and Wittner 1998). For example, Karen Chai (1998) finds that the chance to be with those who have similar cultural backgrounds and experiences is one of SGKAs' main motives for attending the separate SGKA English-language ministries.

Kelly Chong (1998) goes further and finds that participating in ethnic churches reinforces a distinct Korean ethnic identity for SGKAs. She argues that the Korean American Evangelical Protestant community supports the construction of a strong ethnic identity among SGKAs. The ethnic church ideologically defends and legitimates a "set of core traditional Korean values and forms of social relationships" and serves "as an institutional vehicle for the cultural reproduction and socialization of the second-generation into Korean culture" (Chong 1998: 262). Thus, the main component of SGKAs' ethnicity is their parents' Korean culture.

This kind of ethnic retention argument, however, clashes with findings that show that SGKAs' religious services are in many ways distinct from those of the first generation. Studies show that SGKA and other Asian American Evangelicals' religious services are modeled after mainstream Evangelical organizations, not their parents' churches (Alumkal 2002; Jeung 2002; R. Kim 2004).[5] SGKAs also commonly place their Christian identity above their ethnic identity, and some replace their ethnic identity with a broader Christian identity. As David Kyuman Kim writes, SGKA Christians "are becoming grounded, particularly those who have taken on an Evangelical form of faith, in religion that replaces a core 'Korean' identity" (1993: 41). Moreover, Korean church leaders are discovering that many SGKAs are alienated from the first-generation church and are leaving them, a movement dubbed the "silent exodus" (Pai et al. 1987); more than 80 percent of SGKAs are estimated to leave their parents' ethnic church (K. Kim and S. Kim 1996). And one complaint that the SGKAs have against the first generation is that the immigrant church seems more like an ethnic institution than an authentically religious institution (Jeung 2005; R. Kim 2004). Consequently, it is not clear just how much of the first generation's traditional cultures and values constitute SGKAs' own ethnic religious organizations.

Ethnicity and Religion

Multiracial congregations are few and far between. According to the National Congregations Survey and the Survey of Multiracial Congregations, about 90 percent of American religious congregations are racially homogenous (Chaves 1999; Emerson and Smith 2000).[6] Likewise, separate ethnic ministries, rather than multiethnic ministries, are the most popular on college campuses. Segregation, not integration, characterizes America's Christian communities.

In contemporary America, this finding does not just trouble the assimilationists. It disturbs those in religious communities who believe that their religion should be more than a collection of ethnic institutions and should extend beyond the ethnic and racial boundaries that divide the rest of society. It bothers Evangelical Christians who believe that Christians are all "one in Christ." Jesus Christ preached a fundamentally inclusive gospel and desired that his church be united as a "house of prayer for all nations" (Isaiah 56: 7). Evangelical Christians are thus discomfited that the church is more segregated than most other secular institutions in America.

This unease points to the broader tensions that exist between ethnic separatism and religious universalism. Because most religions adhere to some form of universalism, the ethnically separate nature of people's religious participation conflict with their more inclusive religious identity. The tension lies between the desire to stay within the comforts of one's own ethnic community and the desire to take part in the broader religious community. As Raymond Williams writes from his observations on immigrant religious communities in the United States, "the ecumenical is always in tension with the national and the ethnic, as most religious groups appeal to some form of universalism" (1988: 279).

This tension is not strongly felt by newly arrived immigrants whose limited language ability and cultural familiarity in America make it difficult for them to take part in the larger religious community. But it is pronounced for the later generations who do not have such limitations and adhere to a universal faith like Christianity (DeYoung et al. 2003; Jeung 2005). This is the dilemma of SGKA Evangelicals.

As "Evangelicals," Korean American Evangelicals share several theological principles with other conservative Protestants. They believe in the complete reliability and authority of the Bible alone; the divinity of Christ and the efficacy of his life, death, and physical resurrection for the salvation of the human soul; and the importance of conversion and a personal commitment to live according to the commandments of the Bible.[7] Believing that these principles are universally applicable, Evangelicals emphasize sharing their faith with "all nations" and being ultimately united with all ethnic and racial groups through their common faith in Jesus Christ. As a passage in the Bible states: "There is neither Jew nor Greek . . . for you are all one in Christ Jesus" (Galatians 3: 28).[8] This kind of religious belief system conflicts with the separatist nature of Korean American Evangelicals' ethnic religious participation since the ability and option to be more integrative exist, particularly in today's multicultural context (Alumkal 2001; DeYoung et al. 2003; Emerson and Smith 2000; Jeung 2000; Niebuhr 1929).

Despite this conflict between ethnic separatism and religious universalism, separation remains the norm. Sunday mornings are still the most segregated hours of America.

Core Questions

In view of the limitations of assimilation and pluralist theories, as well as the gaps that remain in the literature on ethnicity, religion, and the second generation, this book answers the following questions. What does it means for today's "successful" children of immigrants to incorporate into contemporary America beyond the attainment of socioeconomic mobility? How does the second generation's ethnic identification change—how does it compare with that of their parents, as well as with those in the broader society? What is it about the relationships between ethnicity and religion that makes separation the norm in America's religious communities? These questions are answered through a study of SGKA college Evangelicals' religious participation.

Specifically, the book answers these questions: (1) Why are SGKAs disproportionately joining ethnically exclusive Evangelical campus ministries over pan-ethnic, multiracial, or predominately white campus ministries? (2) How do SGKA Evangelical campus ministries compare with those of first-generation Korean Americans, as well as with other non–Korean Americans' religious communities? (3) How do SGKAs' interactions with the ethnic community and with the broader Evangelical Christian community shape their religious participation? (4) How do SGKAs negotiate the moral and normative tension between ethnic separatism and religious universalism to maintain their ethnic group boundaries?

Why Second-Generation Korean American Campus Evangelicals?

SGKA Evangelicals in college are the focus of this study because they represent a group that is precisely at the juncture of separation versus integration. On the one hand, SGKAs come from an immigrant community where an estimated 70 percent of the population attends an ethnic church. On the other hand, many SGKA college Evangelicals are acculturated and socioeconomically mobile; they have the ability and opportunity to participate in other mainstream Christian congregations and move beyond the ethnic church. This is particularly true since Protestant Christianity has traditionally defined what it means to be American. Being a Protestant is consistent with being American and should facilitate rather than hinder assimilation (Gordon 1964; Yang 1999).

Studying SGKA and other "campus" Evangelicals in the context of a large and diverse university is also appropriate. Newly independent and away from home, students in a large and diverse college setting come in contact with different ethnic groups and have the opportunity to participate in a variety of ethnically diverse religious organizations of their own. By focusing on the college campus, we can also examine various religious organizations within a controlled setting with individuals of similar age and educational status. Additionally, studying the college campus is useful because second-generation Asian Americans and their Evangelical organizations are largely concentrated on college campuses. Moreover, from civil rights to ethnic student movements, college campuses continue to be the locus of new trends, activism, and identity development. Colleges are important arenas of sociopolitical debates, including the topic of ethnic and racial group relations. College is often the first time when students, particularly ethnic minority students, seriously consider notions of ethnicity and race in relation to themselves and others (Kibria 2002). And what develops on the college campus commonly shapes the debates and policies relating to ethnic and racial group relations and foretells what is to come in broader society.

There is also a dearth of research on SGKA and other Asian American campus Evangelicals. Much research and interest has been placed on Asian Americans' educational and occupational attainment, but relatively little is known about their religiosity, particularly on the college campus. Few are aware that the largest Asian American student organizations on college and university campuses are Asian American Christian organizations. As Rudy Busto writes in his observations about the growing numbers of Asian American Evangelicals on college and university campuses, "The lack of empirical data, interpretations, or even acknowledgement of Evangelicalism among Asian American college students is glaring" (1996: 134).

A New Model of Emergent Ethnicity

Instead of assimilation or retention, this book argues that an emergent ethnicity that is constantly "made in the U.S.A." shapes the lives of today's structurally assimilated children of immigrants. I argue that this ethnic formation is not unique to any particular ethnic group but follows the general development of three interactive processes involving microindividual and macrostructural factors:

1. *The Desire for Community x Structural Opportunities* An individual's desire for belonging and community interacts with changes in ethnic density and diversity (the availability of other co-ethnics) to make separate ethnic associations, including separate ethnic religious associations, more possible.
2. *The Desire for Homophily x Imposed Ethnic and Racial Categorizations* Given the choice of a variety of different ethnic group associations, individuals seeking belonging and community at the primary group level will choose what is *most* similar and familiar to them. This homophilic tendency interacts with ethnic and racial categorizations to make separate ethnic identifications and associations more likely.
3. *The Desire for Majority Status x Marginalization* Individuals' desire for power and majority status interacts with ethnic and racial

marginalization to make separate ethnic associations more desirable.

These three interactive processes guide SGKAs' preference for ethnic-specific over pan-ethnic, multiracial, and predominately white campus ministries. Given the structural opportunity to choose from a number of different campus ministries, SGKA Evangelicals will participate in a campus ministry where they (a) can associate with those who are *most* like themselves (those who are *most* likely to share similar familial and cultural experiences); (b) can have the highest likelihood of obtaining power/leadership positions and group dominance; and (c) are least likely to be marginalized as an ethnic or racial group.[9]

Ethnic minorities are not the only ones constructing emergent ethnicities. The same basic three interactive processes that shape SGKAs' emergent ethnicities also explain why whites form a reactive emergent ethnicity. Within an increasingly diverse and multicultural setting where their majority group status seems threatened, whites develop a reactive sense of ethnic groupness. They retreat to separate ethnic organizations of their own where they too can be with those who are most familiar and similar to themselves, are similarly categorized as belonging together, and can maintain their majority status without contest.

All of this does not mean that ethnic group boundaries at the primary group level cannot be crossed. Indeed, they can. Asian Americans' relatively high level of intermarriage, their participation in the growing, albeit few, multiracial congregations all testify to this (DeYoung et al. 2003; Lee and Bean 2003, 2004). But given the structural opportunity to choose, individuals will more likely separate than integrate.

Ethnicity and Religion

Part of why ethnic and racial divisions continue to characterize the Christian community—why Christians can't "all just get along"—is because ethnicity and religion get along so well. Ethnicity and religion perform similar functions and reinforce each other's existence. They both provide meaning and a strong basis for group identity and community. Ethnic religious organizations provide shelter from ethnic and racial marginalization, as well as from secularism. They attract individuals seeking the good in religious and ethnic ties. For these reasons, pursuing separate ethnic ministries becomes the most desirable path for religious leaders.

Data and Research Methods

This case study of SGKA campus Evangelical organizations was conducted at a large and diverse public university campus on the West Coast, which I refer to anonymously as West University (WU). I chose WU because of its sizable Asian American student population, particularly Korean Americans, and its variety of campus Evangelical organizations. Among the growing numbers of Asian American campus Evangelical organizations, Korean American campus Evangelical organizations are the most numerous. There are fourteen different Korean American–related ethnic or pan-ethnic campus Evangelical organizations on the WU campus, and approximately half of the Korean undergraduate student population at WU are involved in Korean Christian ministries.

West University is a large public university with about 30,000 students. Located within one of the most ethnically and racially diverse cities of America, WU is surrounded by various ethnic communities and their respective religious organizations. Reflecting the diversity of its surroundings, WU's student population is approximately 38 percent Asian American, 35 percent white, 15 percent Latin American, and 5 percent African American.[10] Considering WU's size and diversity, the findings of my study should not be generalized to apply to smaller university campuses that are neither as ethnically diverse nor located in a metropolitan area. However, my study of campus ministries at WU will provide a snapshot of what is to come on other major campuses and cities where ethnic and racial diversity is on the rise.

In conducting my research, I first gathered general historical and descriptive data on the growing numbers of Asian American Evangelicals and their organizations using resources available through the internet and the organizations themselves. Additionally, I used data gathered from various informal conversations, a focus group interview, and an e-mail survey with the leaders and administrators of religious communities on campus. I benefited from attending the annual conference of the Association of College and University Religious Affairs (ACURA) and conducting a focus interview with the chaplains, deans, and religious organization coordinators of several university campuses across the United States regarding the growth of Asian American campus Evangelical organizations. My data also include information gathered from an e-mail survey that I sent out to thirty members of ACURA regarding the same topic.[11] After gathering the historical and descriptive data on campus Evangelical organizations in general and Asian American campus Evangelical organizations in particular, I conducted participant observation and 100 personal interviews over a two-year period.

Before conducting in-depth participant observation, I visited most of the Christian campus ministries at WU. Out of the twenty-four Christian campus ministries that I visited, I selected five representative types (six actual groups) of organizations for in-depth field research based on the size, history, ethnicity, and theology of the organizations.[12] They consist of two SGKA campus ministries, which I refer to as the Korean American Mission for Christ (KAMC) and Christian Student Fellowship (CSF);[13] a first-generation Korean American campus ministry, Korea-Campus Crusade for Christ (KCCC); a pan-ethnic Asian American campus ministry, Asian American Christian Fellowship (AACF); a multiracial campus ministry, a chapter of InterVarsity Christian Fellowship (IVCF); and a predominately white campus ministry, a chapter of Campus Crusade for Christ (CCC). I conducted participant observation for two years at these six campus Evangelical organizations to examine SGKA Evangelicals' religious participation.

As a Korean American graduate student in her twenties (at the time of my research) fluent in both Korean and English, I had easy access to the various Christian campus organizations. After introducing myself and informing the leaders of the organizations of my research and receiving permission to conduct my study, I began my participant observation. I examined the worship services and Bible studies, non-religious social activities, organizational structure, and characteristics of the leaders and members of the different organizations.

As a 1.5 Korean American familiar with Evangelical Christianity, I was also able to gain rapport with my research subjects and understand the religious subculture of Evangelicals.[14] Growing up in a family that was involved in a multiracial Evangelical campus ministry helped me to connect with the leaders and members within the campus Evangelical community. While I was familiar with campus Evangelicalism and churches in general, I was unfamiliar with ethnic-specific campus ministries and Korean churches. This, along with my identity as a researcher, helped me to gain some distance and objectivity in my research even as I was able to build rapport and camaraderie with my research subjects.

In addition to participant observation, I conducted 100 personal interviews with the students, as well as the directors, staff, and pastors involved in campus Evangelical organizations. Of the 100 interviews, 50 interviews were conducted with SGKAs involved in Korean American campus ministries;[15] 25 interviews were conducted with SGKAs as well as non–Korean Americans involved in pan-Asian, multiracial, or white-dominant campus ministries; and 25 interviews were conducted with the pastors and staff members of the various campus ministries. Interviews were tape-recorded and lasted between thirty minutes and two hours. After first contacting the leaders of the campus Evangelical organizations, I conducted personal interviews with various members of the organization using the snowball sampling method. I interviewed the staff members and the student leaders of the campus ministry, then the other regular members of the campus ministry based on referrals. I also directly asked students whom I met during my participant observation for interviews.

In the interviews, I first gathered descriptive information about the interview subjects and their religious participation (e.g., place of birth, where they grew up, year in college, past and present religious participation). I then asked them why and how they decided to participate in the campus ministry that they were currently a part of. Those in the Korean American campus ministries were asked why they decided to participate in separate campus ministries over the variety of other campus ministries. The entire set of interview questions is included in Appendix A.

Outline of Chapters

The book is divided into seven chapters, plus a conclusion. Chapter 1 examines the emergence of Asian American Evangelicals and the diversification of the campus Christian community.

Given that seven out of ten Koreans in the United States identify as Christians and are affiliated with an ethnic church, chapter 2 examines the ethnic church background of SGKAs and compares SGKA campus

Evangelicals' religious participation with that of their parents. Chapter 3 then compares SGKAs' campus ministries to those of other first-generation Korean American, Asian American, multiracial, and white majority campus ministries.

Chapters 4 and 5 examine the basis of SGKAs' separate ethnic religious group formation. Chapter 4 answers why the majority of SGKAs choose to participate in separate ethnic ministries in lieu of other pan-ethnic, multiracial, and predominately white campus ministries. Chapter 5 details the substance of the ties that bind SGKAs and examines the factors that unite and separate SGKAs from two ethnic groups that they come into the most contact with: other Asian Americans and whites.

Chapter 6 considers how other ethnic groups', namely whites', interactions with SGKAs and other Asian Americans influence SGKAs' separate ethnic religious participation. Specifically, it addresses why "white flight" takes place when the numbers of Asian Americans increase in a campus ministry and how mainstream campus ministries racially presegregate their organization to separate Asian American students from white students. It shows that whites create their own reactive emergent ethnicity for essentially the same reasons that SGKAs pursue their own ethnic ministries.

Looking at the connections between ethnicity and religion, chapter 7 examines how SGKA Evangelicals work through the tensions between ethnic separatism and religious universalism and maintain separate ethnic group boundaries.

Finally, the concluding chapter summarizes the findings of the book and reflects on what we can expect from SGKA Evangelicals after they leave college.

1

Changing the Face of Campus Evangelicalism

Asian American Evangelicals

More than 95 percent of Americans claim to believe in God, a universal spirit, or life force; nearly 80 percent believe in heaven, and about 70 percent are members of a church or synagogue (Gallup and Lindsay 1999; Kristof 2003). Religion is very much alive in America. The histories of America's founding colleges and universities, however, tell a different story.

Most of the early American colleges and universities were formed to prepare young elite men for the ministry and were linked to Protestant denominations or had some form of Christian patronage (Burtchaell 1998; Hofstadter and Hardy 1952). Since the founding of Harvard in 1636, higher education in the United States was established and functioned within a Christian moral universe where the Christian faith was an essential part of the curriculum, faculty duties, and overall lifestyle (Butler 1989; Hunter 1987). This began to change in the mid-nineteenth century.

Industrialization, urbanization, increasing demand to make education more accessible to the common person, and competition with state-supported schools led many church-affiliated schools to democratize and loosen their ties to religion (McCormick 1987).[1] Pietism, the view that an individual's personal faith is distinct from social learning, along with a growing emphasis on a scientific worldview, further contributed to this change (Marsden 1994; Sloan 1994).[2] As James Tunstead Burtchaell recounts in his book *The Dying of the Light,* on the disengagement of colleges and universities from their christian tradition: "Countless colleges and universities in the history of the United States were founded under some sort of Christian patronage, but many which still survive do not claim any relationship with a church or denomination" (Burtchaell 1998: ix). The disaffiliation of the university from the Protestant church, which began as early as the 1800s, continued into the early 1900s.

Despite the decline and, in some cases, the disappearance of the relationship between the church and the university at the institutional level, the Christian faith survives, primarily through student participation in a variety of voluntary Christian campus organizations.[3] In recent years, many of these organizations have witnessed a revival, as increased numbers of ethnic minorities, particularly Asian Americans, have matriculated into colleges and universities.[4]

Christianity on Campus

Voluntary Student Christian Organizations and Church-Sponsored Ministries

The earliest existing reference to a voluntary student Christian organization in America can be traced to a Christian society at Harvard University in 1706. Although the ethos of colonial colleges was replete with religion, students formed their own voluntary student religious organizations. Meeting weekly, these religious societies focused on the study of the Bible, prayer, and mutual support for living a devout life, and students debated topics on faith and the social issues of the time. These organizations were later joined in the early 1800s by student religious organizations that emphasized missionary work to overseas countries. Due to the continuous influx of students and the dynamics of college life, these groups changed their identities and names year to year and only lasted for a short duration. Nevertheless, voluntary student religious groups can still be found on virtually all American college and university campuses.

Another important thread in the heritage of religion on campus is the Young Men's Christian Association (YMCA) and the Young Women's Christian Association (YWCA). Transplanted from the United Kingdom as an interdenominational Christian organization, the YMCA established programs on college and university campuses of America in 1857 and the YWCA was established in 1886. In contrast to the early student Christian societies that focused on nurturing individuals' religious devotion, providing opportunities for theological debates, and encouraging missionary activities, the Y also emphasized community service projects and embraced a broad range of programs and activities. By 1900, there were 628 campus Y associations in the United States, which were the primary forms of religion on college campuses (Butler 1989). With changing religious expressions in the twentieth century, however, the numbers of Y centers on college campuses began to dwindle; few campus Y centers remain today.

As the university and the church became institutionally separated and new colleges and universities devoid of denominational ties began to form, denominations responded by establishing churches near college towns. These denominational churches near college campuses ran parallel to Christian associations like the Y but distinguished themselves by being designed for students of a particular denomination. The Unitarians created the first of these churches near several college campuses in 1865, followed by the Presbyterians, Methodists, Episcopalians, and Roman Catholics.

One of the distinctive developments of denominationally supported campus ministries is the "Bible chair"—a religious teaching program that the church established at or near a college or university. These Bible chairs provided the teaching of religion at state-supported institutions by particular faith traditions and sought to provide high-quality religious instruction to students. In 1893, the Baptists and Disciples of Christ first established separate Bible chairs at the University of Michigan, and other denominations soon began similar projects on other university campuses (Butler 1989; Shockley 1989). Although denominations and other local churches continue to reach out to college students through campus ministries, the Bible chair pattern of both teaching and ministry ended in the 1960s.[5]

As the Y and the Bible chair movement waned, a new wave of independent campus Christian organizations emerged amid the religious revival that followed World War II.

New Independent Campus Christian Organizations

The post–World War II baby boom, suburban migration, public unease over Communism, and the psychological state of Americans coming out of the Depression and a grief-filled war helped to spur a religious revival. Church attendance and contributions to religious organizations soared. Postage stamps and folded money began to include the phrase "In God We Trust." Americans likewise incorporated the phrase "under God" into the Pledge of Allegiance, and even the popular media adopted Christian themes (Johnstone 2001). Accordingly, virtually all Protestant denominations grew in membership in the 1950s and 1960s.

From 1965 to the present, membership in liberal denominations has declined, but traditionally Evangelical denominations continue to flourish. Since 1965, membership in Evangelical denominations increased at an average five-year rate of 8 percent, and Evangelicalism is one of the fastest growing religious movements in the United States (Hunter 1987: 6). Between 39 and 46 percent of Americans describe themselves as Evangelical or born-again Christians (Gallup and Lindsay 1999).[6]

Coinciding with these changes, many of the growing campus parachurches of today are Evangelical Christian campus organizations. Among others, they include Campus Crusade for Christ (CCC), Inter-Varsity Christian Fellowship (IVCF), Navigators, Fellowship of Christian Athletes, and Jews for Jesus. Evangelical campus organizations have little association with churches and tend to be nondenominational or interdenominational (Butler 1989), but they share several theological principles characteristic of other Evangelical Protestants. They include the belief in (1) the complete reliability and authority of the Bible alone; (2) the divinity of Christ and the efficacy of his life, death, and physical resurrection for the salvation of the human soul; (3) the importance of conversion or being "born again"; (4) having personal faith and "relationship" with Jesus; and (5) sharing their faith with and proselytizing to nonbelievers (Bramadat 2000; Hunter 1983; Marsden 1994; Quebedeaux 1974).

As part of the larger Evangelical movement, campus Evangelical organizations are found on both public and private campuses. They tend to have a chief executive officer or president, who is often also the founder of the organization, along with regional directors and local staff members. The staff members who run the parachurch chapters at the local level are often young, are likely to have been former members of the campus ministry as undergraduates, and tend not to have professional training in ministry. They also raise their own salaries and stress recruiting and mentoring potential new leaders in their campus ministry (Butler 1989; Cherry et al. 2001).

Along with their similarities, there are differences. Each campus Evangelical organization has its own separate programs, national gatherings, and structures of accountability. For example, CCC is known for aggressive evangelism, while IVCF is known more for their "fellowship" and small-group Bible studies. Meanwhile, the Navigators are known for their intensive Bible studies, scripture memorization, and training to build disciples.

With increased matriculation of ethnic minority students, specifically Asian Americans, these and other campus Evangelical organizations have witnessed a change.[7] The face of Christianity at Ivy League and other prestigious college and university campuses has changed from Caucasian to Asian. Traditionally white campus ministries have grown with the surge of Asian American Evangelicals, especially Chinese and Korean Americans, while others have shifted altogether, to become predominately Asian American campus fellowships. Asian Americans are also creating their own ethnic and pan-ethnic campus ministries and have heightened interest in racial reconciliation and multiethnic ministries.[8]

Asian American College Students

In the early 1900s, Asian students in American colleges and universities consisted mostly of foreign-born students along with a small number of U.S.-born Asian students. Although foreign-born Asian students attended a number of colleges and universities across the country, the bulk of the U.S.-born Asians enrolled in the universities along the Pacific Coast (Chan 1991). This pattern changed in the 1960s and 1970s as renewed immigration and an influx of better-educated and higher-income Asian immigrants began to send their children to the top schools in the United States.[9]

The previously invisible and slow-growing population of second-generation Asian American communities began to reverse itself after the late 1960s (Lee and Zhou 2004). The Hart-Celler Act of 1965 abolished the national origins quota system, aiming at a humanitarian goal of family reunification and an economic goal of meeting the demand for skilled labor, and setting an equal 20,000 per-country limit. This enactment, along with global economic restructuring and development in Asia and the failed Vietnam War, signified the beginning of the contemporary Asian American community. Nearly 7 million immigrants from Asia were legally admitted to the United States as permanent residents between 1970 and 2000.

Increased numbers of Asian immigrants and second-generation Asian

Americans coincide with the growth in the numbers of Asian American college students, but disproportionately. The number of Asian American undergraduates on college campuses almost tripled between 1976 and 1986 from 150,000 to 488,000 (Hsia and Hirano-Nakanishi 1989). Then, "Between 1984 and 1995, the numbers of Asian Pacific Americans enrolled in higher education institutions rose 104.5%, with comparable figures of 5.1% for whites, 37% for African Americans, and 104.4% for Hispanics" (Siden 1994: 42). Asian Americans account for roughly 4 percent of the U.S. population. But they make-up more than 15 percent of the student enrollment at Ivy League colleges like Yale, Harvard, and Columbia, and more than 20 percent of the student enrollment at Stanford, the Massachusetts Institute of Technology, and the California Institute of Technology. The numbers are even higher in some of the public universities in California. Over 40 percent of the student enrollment at UC Berkeley, UCLA, and UC Irvine are Asian Americans (Hong 2000; Zhou and Gatewood 2000).[10]

Asian American Student Movements and Multiculturalism

The changes brought on by the civil rights and the ethnic student movements of the 1960s and 1980s helped lay the groundwork that changed colleges and universities to be more multicultural, sensitive to ethnic diversity, and, in certain respects, racially segmented. These developments, along with the continuing rise in ethnic minority student enrollment, have made American higher education more supportive of expressions of ethnic identities and accepting of ethnically-based student groups.

The 1968 San Francisco State College strike spearheaded the ethnic student movement and gave birth to ethnic studies as a regular program offered at various college and university campuses across America. Anti-imperialist wars raging in Asia, Africa, and Latin America; the revolutionary works of Communism; the ideology of international colonialism; racism; and American minorities' lack of political power and agency—all were factors that motivated the strike. The strike was also a direct response to the Master Plan for Higher Education in California in the 1960s, which restricted the admission of minorities and centralized decision-making in the hands of businesses and political figures. The strike articulated ethnic minority students' desire for self-determination

—the right to shape their own history and curriculum, as well as to hire their own faculty. As African American, Asian American, Latin American, and Native American students faced resistance to these requests for self-determination, a campus-wide movement, which was to go down in history as the largest student strike in America, was born.

The strike led to the establishment of the nation's first School of Ethnic Studies at San Francisco State College and marked the birth of the Asian American movement. It set the agenda for articulating Asian Americans' identity, promoting diversity, and challenging white hegemony in higher education. Ethnic student movements and the development of ethnic studies for Asian Americans, as well as for other ethnic groups, countered the cultural domination of the Euro-American knowledge base in American colleges. Ethnic student movements democratized higher education, gave minority students empowerment and self-determination, and helped to create a more multicultural campus setting (Hune 1989).

College campuses have thus become an important arena for broader societal debates on questions of racial equality and justice, and issues of race have been at the center of controversies over curriculum, course content, student admission policies, and faculty hiring (Hune 1989; Kibria 2002; Lee and Zhou 2004). The pull of white assimilation declined. The Western European knowledge base of American higher education was challenged, and multiculturalism, a tolerance of ethnic racial diversity, became more accepted.

Major public universities and the Ivy League schools now offer courses in ethnic history, language, literature, arts, and culture; some have ethnic studies programs for both undergraduate and graduate students. Several university campuses even promote themselves as centers of diversity and multiculturalism. Universities like UCLA state in their general school catalogue that "one of the University's highest priorities is to advance the ethnic diversity of its students, faculty, staff and administrators." At other universities like UC Berkeley, multiculturalism is built into the school's curriculum; incoming students are required to take courses on multiculturalism and diversity. Faculty members of many college and university campuses are also changing, albeit slowly, to reflect an increasingly diverse student body. Today's college and university campuses thus provide students greater opportunities to learn more about their ethnic cultural backgrounds and empower themselves as ethnic groups.

These developments mean that the new generation of Asian American students can experience a cultural awakening (Chan 1991; Hune 1989). Instead of choosing between an "Asian" heritage versus an "American" heritage, the new generation of Asian American students can choose to construct an identity of their own that combines their past history and contemporary circumstances.

Multiculturalism and diversity, however, do not necessarily imply ethnic harmony. A quick glance around the cafeteria and local hangouts on campuses reveal black students sitting separately with other black students, white students clustered with white students, Asian students socializing with other Asian students, and so on. There is more racial segregation than integration. As a student comments: "Just because it is diverse does not mean that everyone is getting along." In fact, precisely because there is greater ethnic awareness and diversity, there may be greater ethnic and racial segmentation on campus.

With these dynamics in mind, we can conclude that the pressure to conform to a presumably unified white majority has declined in many colleges and universities. Matriculating into the major institutions of higher education is not the key marker of assimilation as it once was; instead, it can lead to greater ethnic awareness and mobilization.

Asian American Theology

For the most part, Asian American Evangelicals have adopted the Evangelical theology of their white counterparts. In his ethnographic study of second-generation Chinese American and Korean American Evangelicals, Antony Alumkal finds that Asian American Evangelicals are largely unaware of the Anglo-American roots of Evangelical hermeneutics and treat such beliefs as essential characteristics of Christianity. He writes: "Many second-generation Asian American Evangelicals do not appear to be interested in developing their own contributions to Christian theology. Instead, they remain committed to the theology of American Evangelicalism with little awareness of its roots in Anglo-American culture" (Alumkal 2002: 249). Similarly, Timothy Tseng finds that second-generation Chinese American Evangelicals' biblical interpretations are bound by the European immigrant perceptions of identity construction and a "white American 'Evangelical universalism' that subordinates racial identities" (2002: 251). Asian American Evangelicals thus seem to be doing little if anything to challenge the stereotypical image of Asian Americans as the model minority and offering a viable critique of anti-Asian racism.

Yet, some Asian American theologians are trying to develop an Asian American ministry and theology. There are now both Evangelical and mainline seminaries that offer courses tailored toward Asian Americans. Although native-born Asian Americans are raised in the United States, their religious leaders assert that they are bound by common cultural traditions, beliefs, and values that warrant the creation of separate ethnic or pan-ethnic ministries (Jeung 2005).

In his book *Invitation to Lead: Guidance for Emerging Asian American Leaders*, Paul Tokunaga (2003) (the national coordinator for IVCF's Asian American Ministries) argues that Asian Americans share what he calls an "Asian DNA." Characteristically, Asian Americans, particularly those of East Asian descent, are described as more self-controlled, disciplined, fatalistic, obedient to authority, humble, and collective relative to the European American population. They are thought to be focused on education and economic success, and they experience dealing with dual cultures (Kibria 2002; Lee and Zhou 2004; Min 1999, 2002; Tokunaga 2003). These commonalities are used to explain the need for separate Asian American ministries.

The fact that official denominations recognize Asian Americans as a racial minority further supports the construction of Asian American ministries. For example, mainline seminaries educate seminarians about the specific theological concerns and perspectives of Asian Americans. Asian American social issues, community development, and racial justice are also interests of concern. Additionally, there is an overall sense that religious institutions should take a role in reconnecting Asian Americans with their ethnic and family heritages (Jeung 2002).

All of these developments, along with the increased presence of ethnic minority students, particularly Asian Americans, have led Evangelical campus ministries to be more attuned to ethnic diversity and the needs of ethnic minority students. Campus ministries throughout California and on elite university campuses are evangelizing Asian American students as a distinct group; they offer culturally catered ethnic ministries that institutionally reinforce ethnic boundaries. At the same time, ethnic and pan-ethnic ministries are being formed, discussions of racial reconciliation are becoming popular, and efforts to form multiracial campus ministries are being made. Consequently, there are a variety of ethnically diverse campus ministries in which Asian Americans can potentially take part.

Religious Marketplace

Predominantly white campus Evangelical organizations, along with independent Asian American Evangelical organizations and churches, have created separate ethnic, pan-ethnic, and multiracial campus ministries. Categorizing these different campus ministries is difficult. Campus ministries, like most other student organizations, are constantly in flux, with annual changes in membership and leadership. With this in mind, the different types of ethnically diverse campus ministries in which Asian American Evangelicals, particularly SGKAs, can participate in include ethnic-specific, pan-ethnic, multiracial, and predominately white campus ministries.

Ethnic-Specific Campus Ministries

Ethnic-specific campus ministries that target a single ethnic group can be divided into those that focus on the foreign-born and those that focus on the U.S.-born. Ethnic-specific ministries for the foreign-born are mainly for immigrants and international students who are more comfortable worshipping in their native language. Ethnic-specific campus ministries for U.S. -born Asian ethnic groups are conducted in English and tend to focus on second-generation Korean Americans and Chinese Americans.

Pan-Ethnic Campus Ministries

Pan-ethnic campus ministries for Asian Americans target ethnic groups that are categorized as "Asian American."[11] Most of the pan-ethnic Asian American campus ministries, however, are predominately East Asian American and are likely to have one ethnic group as the majority group. For example, a campus ministry classified as "Asian American" may actually have mostly Chinese American members with only a few other Asian ethnic groups. Additionally, many were formerly ethnic-specific campus ministries that later transitioned into pan-ethnic campus ministries. For example, Little Spark and Asian Baptist Student Koinonia were originally started in the 1980s by Korean Americans, but today they are pan-Asian American Evangelical campus organizations. Little Spark currently has chapters at eight university campuses, while Asian Baptist Student Koinonia has twenty chapters, most of which are on East and West Coast college campuses.

Multiracial Campus Ministries

Relative to ethnic and pan-ethnic campus ministries, multiracial campus ministries are scarce and vary in their diversity. Multiracial campus ministries may have a sizable population of a variety of different ethnic and racial groups, but they may also have one ethnic or racial group as the majority group, along with a smaller number of different ethnic and racial groups. Overall, multiracial campus ministries can be categorized into those that are partially integrated and those that are fully integrated.

Partially integrated multiracial campus ministries have racially integrated large-group gatherings but have additional segregated small-group meetings. For example, all of the different ethnic students may gather together for the main weekly worship services, but some of the ethnic groups (usually the ethnic minorities in the group) will meet separately for small-group Bible studies and fellowship. This is done so that ethnic minority students can have opportunities to have more intimate social interactions with co-ethnics while also getting the experience of worshiping and interacting with a diverse student body.

In contrast to partially integrated multiracial campus ministries, completely mixed campus ministries, which are rarer, have all of the different ethnic and racial groups together for both the large-group and small-group meetings. They try to meet the specific needs of the variety of ethnic and racial groups within a single, unified setting.

White Campus Ministries

In addition, Asian American Evangelicals can participate in a number of mainstream campus ministries that remain predominately white.

These different types of campus ministries can be found across the United States. On a large and ethnically diverse campus like WU, all of the aforementioned types of campus ministries are present.

WU *Campus Ministries*

As previously mentioned, there are five types of campus ministries in my study: two SGKA campus ministries, Korean American Mission for Christ (KAMC) and Christian Student Fellowship (CSF); a first-generation Korean American campus ministry, Korea-Campus Crusade for Christ (KCCC); a pan-Asian American campus ministry, Asian American Christian Fellowship (AACF); a multiracial campus ministry, a chapter of InterVarsity Christian Fellowship (IVCF); and a predominately white campus ministry, a chapter of Campus Crusade for Christ (CCC).

SGKA Campus Ministries: Korean American Mission for Christ and Christian Student Fellowship

KAMC and CSF are two of the largest and well-known SGKA campus ministries at WU. With about a hundred members each, the majority of the members at KAMC and CSF are SGKAs, and their services are conducted entirely in English. Both of these campus ministries have directors and pastors from local churches and seminaries who oversee their organization, but they operate independent of church support and function as student-run organizations. A pastor who graduated from an American seminary and leads an SGKA-based church volunteers his services at KAMC by providing the weekly sermons and general leadership. The director of CSF is a faculty member of a local seminary and pastor of a Korean American church. While he provides overall leadership, the director does not come to the weekly gatherings. Instead, a local seminary student comes to oversee the weekly meetings, and pastors from nearby churches are invited to provide the weekly sermons.

KAMC was founded in the 1970s by a group of first-generation Korean pastors. It was established to incite a "mission movement" among the growing numbers of Korean college students while also helping them build social networks and sort out their bicultural identities as both Koreans and Americans. Because it was started by first-generation Korean Americans, the worship services in KAMC were originally conducted in Korean and consisted of members who were more comfortable speaking Korean than English. In 1993, however, the ministry began to conduct services largely in English. Currently, all of the worship services and Bible studies are conducted in English, and the members are predominately SGKAs. In addition to the chapter at WU, KAMC has five other chapters on university campuses near WU.

Unlike KAMC, CSF focused on SGKAs from its inception. CSF began in 1984 at the WU campus with nine SGKAs who wanted to start a Bible study group for Korean American students who were more comfortable speaking English than Korean. In the late 1990s, CSF changed its formerly ethnic-specific name to a more inclusive non-ethnic specific name—from Korean Christian Fellowship to Christian Student Fellowship. In addition, it began to have ethnically diverse speakers come and provide the weekly sermons instead of regularly having a Korean American pastor or staff member deliver the weekly sermons. CSF has two other chapters at universities near WU.

Although KAMC started as a more first-generation-based Korean campus ministry and CSF was more second-generation focused, both campus ministries became SGKA campus ministries by the late 1990s.

First-Generation Korean American Campus Ministry: Korea-Campus Crusade for Christ

KCCC shares part of its name with one of the largest Evangelical campus parachurches in America, Campus Crusade for Christ. KCCC, however, targets first-generation and 1.5-generation Korean Americans and is officially affiliated with and funded by the CCC headquarters in South Korea.

KCCC was originally founded in Korea with the help of American and British Campus Crusade for Christ, but they now operate independent of them and can be found on numerous college campuses of South Korea.[12] In the year 2000, KCCC had 351 chapters and 16,798 members; these are phenomenal numbers considering that there are a total of 364 colleges in South Korea. Since the 1980s, however, KCCC began sending its own staff members ("missionaries") to the United States to help Korean college students. Established on forty different U.S. college campuses (as of 2006), KCCC targets Korean students who are studying abroad, as well as recently arrived Korean immigrants who are more comfortable speaking Korean than English.[13] Worship services are conducted mostly in Korean, and their staff and financial support comes from Korea. WU KCCC has approximately sixty regular attendants.[14]

Asian American Campus Ministry: Asian American Christian Fellowship

AACF began in 1973 as a campus Bible fellowship for Japanese American college and university students at California State University in Los Angeles. Formerly known as JEMS Campus Bible Fellowship, AACF was originally created for Japanese American students with the support of the JEMS—Japanese Evangelical Missionary Society.[15] From the late 1970s, however, JEMS campus ministry expanded their vision to include others in the Asian American community and started to refer to themselves as the Asian American Christian Fellowship. AACF's goal is "to reach into the university and collegiate community, primarily to those who are Asian Pacific Americans, with a life-changing message of Jesus Christ."[16] With this mission, AACF has nineteen chapters on various college and university campuses along the West Coast. Led by four Asian American staff and additional student leaders, AACF on the WU campus has about 100 members, most of whom are second-generation and later-generation Chinese Americans.

Multiracial Campus Ministry: InterVarsity Christian Fellowship

As an outgrowth of an Evangelical student movement in England, IVCF in the United States was founded in 1938. With about 650 chapters nationwide, IVCF is known for its small- group Bible studies and "fellowship." It is also proactive about diversity and pursuing "racial reconciliation." Accordingly, some of their chapters are multiracial, and one of their most successful multiracial chapters is at WU.

Boasting over 200 members, the racial make-up of WU IVCF reflects the student population at WU with about 40 percent Asians, 40 percent whites, 10 percent Latinos, 5 percent blacks, and 5 percent other ethnic and racial groups. The staff members, who are supported and trained by IVCF headquarters, are also diverse; there are two white, one South Asian American, and two Chinese American staff members.

While the large group meetings of WU IVCF and a few of the small Bible study groups are racially mixed, there are also small-group fellowships that are racially separate. For example, WU IVCF has separate Bible study groups and fellowship gatherings for African American students. WU IVCF can thus be categorized as a partially integrated multiracial campus ministry.

White Campus Ministry: Campus Crusade for Christ

Started by Bill Bright at UCLA in 1951, CCC is an interdenominational campus Evangelical organization that is known for its aggressive evangelism. Active on more than 1,000 college campuses worldwide with about 2,900 full-time campus ministry staff members, it is estimated that CCC shares the gospel with 5 million students a year (as of 2003).[17] Compared with IVCF, CCC is not as proactive about pursuing integrated multiracial ministries.[18] Roughly 90 percent of the fifty or so members that participate in CCC at WU are white. All of the five staff members are white, except for one staff member who is a South Asian American.[19]

Table 1 shows the breakdown.

TABLE I

Types of Ethnic Campus Ministries

Type	Description
Ethnic-Specific Ministries	
First generation	For foreign/international and recently arrived immigrant students; conducted mostly in a foreign language
Second generation (and later generations)	For a U.S.-born or raised ethnic group; conducted entirely in English
Pan-ethnic Ministries	For different ethnic groups categorized as belonging to the same racial group (e.g., Asian Americans)
Multiracial Ministries	
Partially integrated	Part of the organization's gatherings are ethnically and racially integrated, others are not (e.g., large-group meetings are integrated, small-group meetings are not)
Fully integrated	All of the organization's gatherings are ethnically and racially integrated (e.g., both the large-group and small-group meetings are integrated)
White-Majority Ministries	Majority of the members are white Americans

Conclusion

Religion's once strong presence in American higher education has diminished and in some cases altogether disappeared at the institutional level. Despite the secularization of religion at the institutional level in colleges and universities, religion lives on through students' participation in a variety of voluntary religious organizations. And in recent years, the campus Christian community has witnessed a revival with the growth in the numbers of Asian American Evangelicals.

Increased presence of ethnic minorities, particularly Asian Americans, along with changes brought on by ethnic student movements and multiculturalism, have led to the construction of a range of ethnically diverse campus ministries. Accordingly, on a large university campus like WU, a SGKA seeking religious community has many choices. He or she can choose to participate in an ethnic, pan-ethnic, multiracial, or predominately white campus ministry. Given that SGKAs have such choices, the next chapters examine why most SGKA Evangelicals flock to separate ethnic ministries and detail how SGKAs' religious participation compares with that of the first generation, as well as that of their non–Korean American Evangelical peers.

2

Second-Generation Korean American Evangelicals and the Immigrant Church

It is hard to find a Korean immigrant who is not involved in a church. At least 70 percent of over a million Koreans in the United States identify themselves as Christians and regularly attend the 3,500 or so Korean churches every Sunday (Hurh and K. Kim 1990; J. Kim 2002; Min 2000). Accordingly, to understand SGKAs' religious participation, we have to study the immigrant ethnic church and the second generations' connection to it.

Korean Immigration and the Ethnic Church

Approximately a quarter of Korea is Christian. In the United States, however, near three-quarters of Koreans are Christians and are affiliated with an ethnic church. Wherever there is a group of Korean Americans, one can expect that there will be a Korean church nearby. The significance of the ethnic church in the lives of Korean Americans is evident in each of the different waves of Korean immigration in the United States.

First Wave (1903–1950)

The story of Korean immigration in America begins with the arrival of 102 Koreans in Honolulu, Hawaii, on January 13, 1903[1] (Abelmann and Lie 1995; Choy 1979; Hurh and K. Kim 1990; Park 1997). Between 1903 and 1905, more than 7,226 Koreans arrived in Hawaii to work in its sugar plantations. Many of these early Korean immigrants are suspected to have been peasants or semiskilled urbanites from fairly developed metro and port cities in Korea that were also the sites of massive Christian conversions (Chan 1991; Hurh and K. Kim 1990; J. Kim 2002). A significant number of Korean emigrants were also mobilized by Protestant missionaries to journey to the United States. Accordingly, it is not surprising that roughly 40 to 60 percent of the Koreans who arrived in the United States before 1905 were Christians and that Korean churches were soon formed upon their arrival (I. Kim 2004; J. Kim 2002).

In November 1903, within the first few months of settlement, Korean laborers formed the Hawaii Methodist Church, and in February 1905, the Hawaii Korean Anglican Church was formed. By 1905, there were seven Korean Christian chapels in Hawaii. The Koreans who ventured onto the mainland also established churches, including the San Francisco Korean Methodist Church formed in 1903 and the Los Angeles Presbyterian Church founded in 1905. By 1950, there were approximately sixty Christian churches serving Koreans in Hawaii and the mainland (Cho 1984; I. Kim 2004; J. Kim 2002).

With one out of ten Korean immigrants being female, the sex ratio among Korean laborers was not as skewed as was the case for the Chinese and Japanese laborers at the time. With the arrival of a little over a thousand Korean women who entered as picture brides, women made up 21 percent of the adult Korean population in the United States by 1920 (Kwon et al. 2001). The presence of women facilitated the development of families and the formation of Korean churches in the United States.

With the passage of the Immigration Act of 1924, which prohibited the entrance of Asian immigrants (also known as the Oriental Exclusion Act), no official immigration took place from Korea between 1924 and 1950. As strangers in a new land cut off from home, particularly with the Japanese annexation of Korea, the early wave of Korean immigrants were isolated. Moreover, until the passage of the McCarran Walter Act in 1952, Korean-born individuals were not allowed to become naturalized U.S. citizens.

Unable to fully engage themselves as U.S. citizens and troubled over the Japanese colonization of Korea, Korean Americans actively involved themselves in homeland politics and advocated Korea's independence from Japan. In this process, Korean Christian churches became important sites for political activism and nationalism by Korean immigrants.[2] The separation of church and state found in mainstream America was not evident in the early Korean church. Homeland politics commonly intermingled with religion.[3]

In addition to being the locus of political activity, Korean churches operated as the main community centers that addressed the various survival needs of their congregants. They provided multiple services and programs to ease Korean immigrants' settlement in the new country, including job placement, counseling, legal aid, language classes, interpretation and translation, among others (J. Kim 2002). Moreover, the churches served as a "home away from home" where fellow Korean exiles could find emotional and social support. At the ethnic church, immigrants could speak their native language, exchange stories from back home, seek the advice and assistance of fellow co-ethnic church members, and support each other through the difficulties of working at the sugar plantations. The Korean church thus functioned as the educational, cultural, political, and social service center for Koreans. It also became the representative of the Korean community to the rest of U.S. society.

Second Wave (1951–1964)

Impelled by the Korean War, the second wave of Korean immigrants consisted mostly of wives of U.S. servicemen (6,423), orphaned adoptees (5,348), and a few refugees, professionals, and students (Hurh and K. Kim 1984). The stories of the Korean wives of American GIs and war orphans are not well-documented in the history of Korean America (Yuh 2004). The experiences of these two silenced groups are considered to be secondary in and outside of the Korean American community, and the two groups did not provide a fertile basis for the development of ethnic churches (J. Kim 2002).[4]

Very little is also documented about the estimated 5,000 students who came to the United States between 1950 and 1965. But it is known that U.S. missionaries had an active role in recruiting these Korean students to study in the United States in the hopes that they would propagate Christianity. For example, "At the time of the political and economic upheaval in the divided Korea, many (male) Koreans made the decision to put their souls in the hands of U.S. missionaries in exchange for a ticket to the 'land flowing with milk and honey'" (J. Kim 2002: 195). Survival and faith were thus interlinked.

Third Wave (Post-1965)

During the ideological competition of the Cold War, racist immigration laws that favored European immigration and excluded Asian immigration became somewhat of an embarrassment to the U.S. government. This, along with the need for skilled labor, led to the passage of the Hart-Cellar Act of 1965, which abolished the national origins quota system and aimed to unify families and draw skilled laborers into the United States. After this enactment, nations outside of the Western hemisphere were permitted to send up to 20,000 emigrants per year, with immediate relatives of U.S. citizens not subject to numerical limitations. The family reunification provisions, however, were actually intended to facilitate the immigration of Europeans, who had the most relatives in the United States. Despite the original intension of the provisions, immigration from Asia increased dramatically, while immigration from Europe unexpectedly fell in the 1970s (I. Kim 2004; Warner and Wittner 1998).

Changes in immigration law, along with the forced modernization programs under the dictatorial regime of General Park Chung Hee of Korea, led many Koreans to emigrate in the 1960s. General Park, who later became president of Korea (1961–1979), pushed Korea away from its traditional role as an agricultural nation and moved the country toward world capitalism and export-oriented industrialization. Successful industrialization and economic development, however, went hand in hand with social dislocation and polarization of the rich and poor. Park's regime favored large business conglomerates (*chaebols*) and the elite segment of Korean society at the expense of the lower and middle strata. The rural population became impoverished, smaller businesses weakened, white-collar workers became frustrated, and various civil rights were violated. In this context, many Koreans with the means to emigrate, namely middle-class Koreans, left for the United States in search of better lives.

From 1970 to 1980, the Korean population in the United States increased by 412 percent, and Korea has consistently been on the list of the top ten immigrant-sending countries since the 1980s (USINS 1997). The Korean American population increased from 69,150 in 1970 to 1,076,872 in the year 2000. Koreans are currently the fifth-largest Asian group behind the Chinese, Filipinos, Vietnamese, and

South Asians. According to the 2000 U.S. Census, Koreans made up 0.38 percent of the U.S. population and 10.5 percent of the non-Hispanic Asian and Pacific Islander population (Reeves and Bennett 2004).

In the 1990s, however, Korean immigration to the United States dropped as Korea advanced socioeconomically and as stories of the 1992 Los Angeles riots and the struggles of Korean immigrants became more commonplace. The numbers of Korean immigrants fell from an average of 35,000 per year in the late 1980s to fewer than 15,000 per year in the mid-1990s. This shift, along with natural population growth, contributed to the declining foreign-born Korean population in America. In 1990, about 82.2 percent of the Korean population in the United States was foreign-born. Estimates drawn from the 1998 and 2000 Current Population Surveys show that foreign-born Koreans comprised approximately 52.4 percent of the Korean American population, the second generation made up 21.9 percent, and the third and later generations were 25.7 percent of the Korean population (Logan et al. 2001).

While the numbers of Korean immigrants have declined, Korean churches continue to be dominated by the first generation. The leadership positions in the Korean American faith communities are monopolized by the first generation and are handed down to the new immigrants from Korea, not the SGKAs (Kwon et al. 2001). With this in mind, we now turn to the current state of Korean immigrants and their churches in America.

Korean Churches Today

Like the early wave of Korean immigrants at the start of the twentieth century, the recent waves of Korean immigrants consist of a large number of Christians. Half of the Koreans leaving for America in the post-1965 era were Christian, and surveys conducted in the 1980s show that almost three-quarters of the Korean immigrant population in America identified themselves as Christians and attended mostly Protestant churches (Hurh and K. Kim 1984, 1990). In some cities, the numbers are higher. A 1997–1998 survey conducted by Pyong Gap Min reported that 79 percent of Korean immigrants in Queens, New York, identified themselves as Christians, and 83 percent of them reported that they attend an (ethnic) church once a week or more (Min 2000). While studies show that Korean immigrants tend to "church-hop" and are unlikely to stay within a single church for an extended period, the vast majority of Korean immigrants in America attend ethnic churches throughout their lives. Many are also willing to drive long distances to attend church and tend to be extensively committed to their church (W. Kim and K. Kim 1990).

Defying the stereotype that Asians are mostly Buddhists, the Korean immigrant community in the United States is thus largely a Protestant Christian population that faithfully attends church. What then makes this the case—what contributes to Korean Americans' religious vitality in America? The Korean American community is heavily Christian due to the selective migration of the more Westernized and Christianized middle-class Koreans, as well as their religious conversion after migration. But the community is considerably Christian and church-going also because immigrant churches continue to function as the center of the Korean community.

The ethnic church provides various forms of emotional and social support for recently arrived immigrants finding their way in a new country. One of the ways that they do this is by helping immigrants regain the social status that they lost in the process of immigrating and adapting to a new land (Hurh and K. Kim 1984; I. Kim 1981; Min 1992). Due to language limitations, cultural unfamiliarity, and other disadvantages, many contemporary Korean immigrants cannot maintain the professional, administrative, and managerial positions that they once had in Korea. In this situation, the ethnic church helps alleviate immigrants' status depreciation and depravation by giving them recognition and opportunities to take on leadership positions within the church.

Various practical social services are also available in the ethnic church. In their study of Korean Christian churches in Houston, Texas, Victoria Kwon and her colleagues found that ethnic churches provide "aid in buying a vehicle, and finding housing . . . baby-sitter referrals, social security information, and translating services; making airport pickups; visitations for new babies and hospitalized members; registering children for school; applying for citizenship; dealing with the courts" (1997: 261). Moreover, the ethnic church functions as an important source of social capital. Ethnic entrepreneurs whose businesses cater to the co-ethnic community find the ethnic church to be a particularly valuable place for conducting business and gaining a reliable clientele base. In a study of the New York Korean community, Ilsoo Kim (1981) found that some Korean entrepreneurs even hold multiple memberships in several Korean churches to expand their networks for business purposes. Those who receive services from these business entrepreneurs can also benefit; they can be assured that they will be treated fairly by the businesses since news of dishonesty or improper business can spread quickly within a tight ethnic religious community. Those seeking employment can also get news of potential employment from businessmen and businesswomen within the ethnic church.

In addition to practical social services, religion and religious organizations assist immigrants' social psychological adjustment in the new country by providing them a sense of meaning, comfort, and belonging. Due to the uncertainties of sojourning or migrating to a foreign land, migration becomes a "theologizing experience": "Loneliness, the romanticizing of memories, the guilt for imagined desertion of parents and other relatives, and the search for community and identity in a world of strangers [brought] . . . formidable psychic challenges" to the new immigrants (Smith 1978: 174). In this situation, religion and its organizations become important sources of comfort and meaning.

A conservative Protestant faith also provides Korean immigrants an absolute belief system and a clear moral standard in an otherwise volatile existence as immigrants (W. Kim and K. Kim 2001; Yang 1999). Moreover, ethnic churches operate as extended families—a place where immigrants can find familiar faces, food, sounds, and smells in a new land. Korean churches provide the social cultural space where Korean immigrants can regularly come together and practice traditional Korean customs and norms and speak their native- tongue, wear traditional Korean clothes, and celebrate Korean holidays.

Additionally, Korean Americans' religious vitality can be attributed to the syncretism between traditional Korean culture and Protestant Christianity. The centrality of moral, social, and family values in Confucianism complements the moral codes and teachings of conservative Protestant Christianity. The Christian churches' stance against moral depravity and the importance of honoring and obeying one's parents, and the promotion of male domination, are in many ways congruent to patriarchal Confucianism.[5]

The Second Generation

Background

Most of the SGKA students in my study came from middle-class backgrounds and grew up in ethnically diverse cities surrounding the university. Some attended grade schools where the majority of the students were Asian American. Others went to schools where Latin and African American students were the majority, and still others grew up in schools where white students were the majority in number. Reflecting their school backgrounds, SGKAs in my sample had ethnically and racially diverse groups of friends: 40 percent had mostly an ethnically diverse group of friends; 24 percent had mostly Asian American friends; 24 percent had mostly white friends; and 10 percent had mostly Korean American friends.

While SGKA's neighborhoods, schools, and friends were ethnically diverse, their religious experiences were, for the most part, homogenous. All of the fifty Korean American students in Korean American campus ministries that I interviewed had attended a Korean church (whether regularly or irregularly), and a few had served in leadership positions. Most of them were involved in a church that one or both of their parents attended. The fact that the first and the second generations both went to the same church, however, did not mean that they had the same religious experiences.

The first generation's religious beliefs and practices no doubt influence those of the second generation, but they do not guarantee that the second generation will follow suit and participate in separate ethnic religious organizations like the first generation does. Part of the reason for this is that the SGKAs' religious participation is in many ways unlike the first generation's religious participation. Even if some may have sat through the main services with the rest of the Korean-speaking first generation, much of their religious participation was experienced in separate English ministries specifically tailored to the second generation. These separate services are led by 1.5 or SGKA pastors and staff or even by some non-Korean Evangelicals who are trained in American seminaries, in contrast to the first-generation's services, which are led by pastors trained in Korea (Chai 2001).

The fact that most SGKAs cannot speak Korean fluently also makes it practically difficult for them to take part in the first generation's religious services and remain connected to the immigrant church. Studies further show that SGKA and other Asian American Evangelicals' religious services are modeled after mainstream Evangelical organizations, not first-generation churches (Alumkal 2002; Jeung 2002; D. Kim 1993). These developments have led some scholars to refer to the ethnic church as a "de facto congregation" where the second-generation ministry has "different styles, priorities, and visions for the future" than the first generation has (Chai 1998: 302).

The rift between the first and the second generations' religious participation is also evident in the departure of many SGKAs from the first-generation church. SGKAs accompany their parents to church in their youth but later leave their parents' church once they are in college.[6] It is estimated that more than 80 percent of the second generation leave their parents' church (Cha 2001; Chai 2001; K. Kim and S. Kim 1996). Church leaders have dubbed this outward drift as the "silent exodus" because much of it goes unnoticed by the first generation and because the numbers are staggering. Others describe the phenomenon as the "church of family members" becoming the "church of parents" (Song 1994). More recent studies on the topic show that the church attrition rate among the second generation is not as dramatic as the church leaders suggest (Chai 2001). Nevertheless, many SGKAs do not view the immigrant church as their own and are leaving them.

Sources of Division

Much of the division between the first and the second generations' religious participation comes from generational and cultural differences. SGKAs characterize the first generation's religious participation as hierarchical, patriarchal, and static, and they describe their own as democratic, egalitarian, and dynamic. An SGKA pastor who has worked as a liaison in the Korean church between the two generations describes the differences by pointing to the varying emphases placed on titles and hierarchy:

> The first-generation is into distinctions, they are title-oriented . . . for example, *gip san nim* [the Korean word for deacon] means servant, but the Korean interpretation of that is like a higher stage of being religious, more reverential, more honorific. But the second generation do not view it that way, once you are done serving, you discard the title; being a deacon is more functional.

Unlike their parents, the second generation are not so preoccupied with titles and hierarchy and tend to choose their religious leaders based on ability rather than age and status, as the pastor continues to elaborate:

> The first generation see authority by virtue of age. In our first-generation congregation, we have 200 members and 209 are deacons! That is over 100 percent! But with the second-gen[eration] ministry, we have about 150 to 200 English-speaking SGKAs and we have three deacons, and we do not appoint deacons according to age but by what they have done, which is more in line with American culture.

The pastor thus explains that the second generation are more Americanized and are not as hierarchical as the first generation. Along these lines, SGKAs point out that SGKA pastors and staff are "more approachable" and that they are more likely to refer to them by their first names than by their religious titles. An SGKA explains, "The second-generation pastors are more approachable; . . . my pastor prefers that I just call him Joe."

Intergenerational and intercultural differences between the first and the second generations are also evident in the two groups' views on gender roles. Whereas the women in the first-generation ethnic churches are placed in subservient and subordinate positions, they are full participants in the second-generation campus ministries. An SGKA student leader of KAMC describes the difference in this way:

> How is the first and the second generation different? Definitely, the role of the women. . . . The first-generation church puts women in a very powerless position. They don't have a real voice in the church, and I don't think they are much regarded as part of the church, while the second gen[eration] tend to realize that women have to be recognized as definitely part of the church.

Other women, especially the young women, share the view that the immigrant churches leave them feeling stifled, limited, and pressured to assume traditional gender roles. For instance, a young woman describes how the pastor of an immigrant church she used to attend responded to her excitement about pursuing an academic career:

I was telling him all of the things I was excited about—my vision of being an academic, about my New Testament class, history courses in religion, and I was starting to open up about studying abroad—and I was talking and then he grabbed my hand and said, "You know a woman's very highest calling is to be a mother." I listened, but I was so disappointed. The sad thing is that it is not so rare to hear things like that.

Another Korean American woman explains that compared with the first generation, the second generation are more egalitarian in their gender relationships: "First-generation churches think that if you want to be a good mom you have to stay home and take care of the kids, but the second-gen[eration churches] are definitely more aware that we can't always choose that. Just because you work doesn't mean that you are a bad mother. . . . The second-gen[eration] are less tradition-bound in that way."

Intergenerational and intercultural divisions between the two generations also extend beyond social status and gender roles. Many children of Korean immigrants note that the first generation's religious participation is more static, antiquated, and inexpressive than their own, as an SGKA explains: "When I sit in the regular Sunday worship with the adults [older immigrants] . . . it is boring, not very exciting, but [the second generation] are more likely to hit people with something they are not expecting . . . like throw in a skit, maybe even a movie, maybe a hip-hop dance, mix it up more. It's just so much more fun and creative." Another student similarly adds,

> The first-generation is very dry. . . . Their worship services are very quiet, not a lot of emotions. . . . They just sit there, listen, and leave. . . . And the speakers are first-gen[eration] Koreans, just stone-faced and straightforward. But for us there is a mix of emotion and rational thought, and I think in that sense there are a lot of differences. We get lively and we have drums in our praise, not just an organ and singing hymns. We have guitar, bass, keyboard, . . . and the speakers are a lot of times more exciting.

Live music from Vineyard, Hosanna Music Groups, and Integrity played on keyboard, bass, drums, and guitar provide a striking contrast to the quiet and solemn atmosphere and a single monotonous organ with "boring hymnals" in Korean immigrant churches. Except for the lyrics of the songs, "praise" resembles a pop concert. The room is dimly lit, lights flash only on stage, and the praise leader has an electric guitar strapped across his chest and sings loudly into the microphone. Accompanying the praise leader is a drummer, electric bass and keyboard players, and a superior sound system. At a special "praise night" where one of the best local praise bands came to "lead the worship," one student turned to his neighbor and asked, "Don't they sound like Pearl Jam?"[7] SGKAs' worship is far more dynamic and contemporary than the subdued worship of their immigrant parents.

In these ways, SGKAs commonly define their religious participation in opposition to that of the first generation. The first generation's religious participation is characterized as hierarchical, patriarchal, and static, while the second generation's religious participation is described as democratic, egalitarian, and dynamic. For this reason, we can deduce that SGKAs' religious organizations formed in large part as a reaction against what they disliked about the first generation's religious participation and stems from the intergenerational and intercultural conflicts that they have with their immigrant parents.

The divisions between the first and second generations also reflect the second-generation's questions about the religious authenticity of their parents' churches.

In Search of Religious Authenticity

The second generation allege that immigrant churches are factious and not "biblical" or "religious" enough. Citing the frequent internal political battles and subsequent splitting off within immigrant churches as prime examples, many SGKAs explain that the churches they had once attended with their parents have since divided. An SGKA student recounts how several lay leaders physically fought with one another over a dispute regarding which pastor to hire: "Korean churches, what are they known for? Splitting. They are all splitting, practically everyone here experienced it. . . . And it is one thing if they are splitting because they want to spread God's words in other places, . . . but it is mostly political, like we don't like that pastor or you guys are not giving us respect . . . or money conflicts." There is a running joke among SGKAs, which goes, "Let's make like a Korean church and split." The punch line is that the most effective way to get students going and moving is to replicate the behavior of a Korean church, that is, to split.[8] The internal political battles and frequent splitting, combined with the preoccupation with status, make immigrant ethnic churches appear more like ethnic than religious institutions.

In addition, some SGKAs contend that their parents are not very serious about Christianity and spreading the gospel. For example, while immigrant parents encourage their children to attend church, they often disapprove of them becoming "too religious," especially at the cost of their careers, as a Korean American college student expresses: "It is like they dropped me off at Sunday school to pick up good values, but did not expect me to really take [my religion] seriously, so when I said I wanted to be a missionary to China, they were like whoa. . . . No way, you are going to med school." Another Korean American student adds, "My Dad tells me go to church, but don't get too serious about it." From the perspective of the second generation, these parental concerns contradict the very tenets of the Evangelical Christian faith which challenge individuals to be serious about their faith and put "Jesus first above all else."

SGKAs further note that their immigrant parents' churches are ethnically exclusive and too self-contained, which they feel makes the churches religiously unauthentic. To illustrate this, an SGKA campus ministry staff who grew up in an immigrant church describes the following incident:

> One time these neighborhood Latino kids wanted to come out to our church . . . and they came up to the courtyard [near a table full of after-church refreshments], and this old grandma Korean deaconess started yelling at the Latino kids, yelling at them that the donuts are not for them, . . . so I was like what is going on here? So I gave them the donuts and she gave me this dirty look. I took these kids to the elementary group [which is held in English], and they came every week after that. I mean, they so wanted to hear God's words. If you don't want to affect the community, what are you doing? The church should be a place where the whole neighborhood [is] affected, . . . otherwise, are they really doing God's work?

From the perspective of the second generation, the ethnic exclusivity in first-generation churches and their lack of involvement in local communities seem opposed to Jesus' command to "love one's neighbor," practice charity, and preach the Gospel "to all nations." SGKAs thus question the religious authenticity of first-generation churches.[9]

Conclusion

This chapter examined the intimate connection between Korean immigration and the ethnic church. It also considered how SGKAs, many of whom grew up in the immigrant church, compare their religious participation to that of their parents. In so doing, we found that both generations may enter the same church, but they do not come out of it with the same religious experience.

The second generation view their parents' religious services and organizations as hierarchical, patriarchal, and static, while they view their own worship services as more democratic, egalitarian, and dynamic. Indeed, their religious services are modeled after American mainstream Evangelical organizations instead of immigrant churches; they are conducted in English, are led by pastors who are trained in American seminaries, and are more "Americanized." The second generation further complain that the first generation's church lacks religious authenticity and say they seek a more authentic religious experience.

Accordingly, SGKA campus ministries are formed in part as a reaction *against* their parents' church. They are created in response to what the SGKAs found wanting in their parents' churches, which is spurred on by intergenerational and intercultural conflicts that they have with the first generation.

3

Korean American Campus Ministries in the Marketplace

As early as 7 A.M., students from numerous campus ministries sign up for the best spot on the popular walkway on campus to set up their tables and disseminate information on their organization. They pass out bright flyers and give out free food and school supplies with promises of good fellowship, salvation, and even a future spouse. As one of the campus ministry representatives characterizes it, the walkway is like "a busy market except that all of the vendors are campus ministries."

In this diverse marketplace, what makes SGKA campus ministries stand out? How do they compare to the first-generation Korean American as well as to the other pan-Asian American, multiracial, and predominately white campus ministries?

Comparing Campus Ministries: Similarities

Access

Any interested student can obtain a list of the campus ministries and their contact information through the university's student resources website, as well as through a list of campus ministries available at the WU Student Center. One can also contact any of the six different campus ministries during the beginning of the school year when they set up their tables on campus to draw new members. Throughout the school year, advertisements for the different campus ministries can be spotted on the big poster boards set up on the popular walkways and on the flyers posted around campus.

It is also possible for one to simply walk through the campus on weeknights from 6 to 10 P.M. and be drawn to a campus ministry's worship service by the sound of music, chatter, or preaching. I was able to find where Korean American Mission for Christ (KAMC) was meeting following the sound of people singing praise songs. Some campus ministries even have students stand or sit behind a table in front of the lecture halls to greet and guide the attendees.

Additionally, all of the six campus ministries in my study meet on or near walking distance from campus on weekdays. As one of the largest campus ministries at WU, IVCF has two separate weekly gatherings: one focuses on freshmen and sophomore students, and the other focuses on junior and senior students. The former has about 100 or more attendees and meets on campus on Tuesdays; the latter meets near campus on Thursdays at the apartment of several IVCF staff members and has about half as many attendees. The rest of the five campus ministries have just one weekly large-group gathering. KAMC and AACF meet every Wednesday between 5 and 6 P.M. in lecture halls. CCC meets on Tuesdays at 7:30 in one of the large study rooms at the WU Student Center. CSF and KCCC meet on Thursdays at 6 P.M. in lecture halls.[1]

Praise

One of the common responses to the question of why churches are so racially segregated is that racial groups worship differently, particularly through music. As a pastor of a multiracial church writes, "music shouldn't be classified stereotypically, but ministry leaders need to be aware that many people do associate certain genres with race" (Anderson 2004: 109). Most commonly, black Christians have a distinctive way of singing gospel songs that separates them from other Christians. In the case of the six campus ministries, however, worshipping through songs, commonly referred to as "praise," is largely similar.

Praise is held toward the beginning of the weekly gatherings for thirty minutes to an hour as students trickle into the service. A band consisting of guitar, bass, drums, and/or keyboard enthusiastically leads praise at the spot where the professors usually lecture. With lyrics of songs from Vineyard, Hosanna Music Groups, and Integrity projected on screen, there is at least one person with a guitar leading a contemporary style of praise. The lights are dimmed as students move their bodies to the rhythm of the music. The atmosphere of the room is often like that of a pop concert.

At CSF's weekly gathering, a male student in a tight T-shirt and loose jeans leads the praise band with an electric guitar strapped across his chest. He sings with a deep resounding voice while vigorously strumming his guitar. After a while, he sings more softly with his eyes closed as he holds the microphone close to his mouth. Meanwhile, the room is darkly lit except for the projected lyrics on a screen. A crowd of about a hundred casually dressed students sings standing up. Some sing softly, while others sing loudly, passionately moving their bodies and clapping to the rhythm of the music. After about forty-five minutes, the lead singer of the praise band prays and ends the praise.

On another weeknight, KAMC's praise is led by a male student on electric guitar accompanied by another male drummer, bass guitar player, and a female keyboarder. The praise music sounds like rock music, but the lyrics mention Jesus (e.g., "what a friend we have in Jesus"; "it is all about you, Jesus"; and "we break down every idol and worship you"). While the band leads the praise, some in the crowd lift up their hands as they sing. Others stand swaying side to side with their eyes closed. When the music gets more upbeat and the drums and electric guitar pick up, students clap their hands and some jump up and down to the rhythm of the music. After about thirty minutes to an hour of singing, the praise leader prays for the group and signals the end of praise.

CCC's praise band consists of two white men on guitars and another white man on bass. The praise band is led by a man who was formerly a member of a rock band. Dressed in faded jeans and a T-shirt, the praise leader sings softly, moving his body to the rhythm of the music as the crowd of about forty to fifty students sing along. CCC also closes their praise with prayer. KCCC's praise band includes another woman on keyboard and a man on bass and is more upbeat, but the format of praise is the same.

In contrast to the above campus ministries, IVCF's praise band, like their overall membership, is racially diverse. A white man leads praise with an African American woman on the electric keyboard, two Asian American men on bass and guitar, and another white woman controlling the overhead with the lyrics to the praise songs.[2] The songs that are sung are similar to those of the KAMC, CSF, and CCC, but IVCF members also sing some of the praise songs in Spanish with English subtitles. The overall style of praise, however, is similar to the other Evangelical campus ministries. While the music plays, some of the students dance and put their hands in the air and clap like the students at KAMC and CSF. The end of IVCF's praise is also signaled with prayer.

AACF's praise band consists of an electric guitarist, bass player, drummer, and keyboarder. The lead singer is dressed in tattered jeans and a surfer T-shirt; he is accompanied by two female back-up singers. Their praise is also followed by prayer. The only real difference is that AACF's praise is conducted further into the evening's program.

The fact that all of the campus ministries participated in a university-wide praise gathering where a famous Christian musician came to lead praise also indicates that the style of praise among the campus ministries is alike. Approximately 60 percent of the students at the special praise event were Asian, with the second largest group being whites. The guest celebrity praise leader, however, was white, as were most of his accompanying band members.

Sermons and Testimonies

As Evangelical campus ministries, the sermons and personal testimonies shared in worship services are similar in content and touch on three main interconnected themes.

First, the sermons encourage students to work on their personal relationship with God/Jesus.[3] Students are reminded to pray, read the Bible, and spend "quiet time" with God.[4] The sermons talk about God's love, grace, righteousness, judgment, and mercy, and they encourage students to strengthen their faith and relationship with God despite the various temptations they may face.

For example, a young pastor and a former CSF alumnus, Pastor Mark, speaks at one of CSF's weekly meetings about the importance of being a "real" and "mature" Christian.[5] He asks the audience, "How mature are you as a Christian? How passionate are you? How would you do on the SAT, the Spiritual Achievement Test?" The following is an excerpt from Mark's sermon:

> Are you making higher standards? Because that is an indicator of your maturing. Are you guys going to places because you know you have freedom, places that you should not be going to? How important is your church to you? Are you just hanging out at WU on a Friday night, or are you taking the two hours to go to church? How committed are you? Are you going to clubs or pubs instead of going to church and

serving? Saying that we have no time is not an excuse. God calls us to be mature, we can not put our feet in two worlds. . . . Don't neglect your spiritual life and just be status quo.

Pastor Mark thus instructs the students to overcome various temptations and alternative lifestyles and be committed followers of God.

On another night on the other side of campus, a South Asian IVCF staff member named Jerome interweaves his personal testimony with a sermon on the importance of having a strong relationship with God. After introducing himself as an IVCF staff of two years who graduated from WU as a chemistry major, Jerome talks about his religious background and experience:

I grew up in an orthodox church, very traditional Church of Saint Thomas, where they have chants and are very traditional and liturgical. I followed the tradition of the church, the creed, Lord's Prayer, which I recited. For me, following God was just adhering to tradition and liturgy. But what Jesus ultimately desires is to be in a close relationship with his people, just like a friend. I used to go through the Christian motions, but now my life with Jesus is so much better than what I had in high school. I didn't have to chant theology, Jesus broke the tradition and rules and I had purpose, real friendship with God. What about you? Is it more than just rules?

Jerome then talks about how his parents wanted him to stay home and take an internship after he graduated. Instead, Jerome said he went to an inner city (to take part in the IVCF urban ministry) to "work for God" and "build a fully solid relationship" with him. When he did this, Jerome confesses, God "totally hooked [him] up." His future life direction was clear, and he was overjoyed because he had given up his internship and placed God first in his life.

Second, sermons discuss how students should relate to others as Christians. For example, Pastor Kwon from KCCC talks about how it was possible for him to stay married for eighteen years because both he and his wife feel "sufficient with God's love." He concludes that we can truly love others and have strong relationships only if we first know and accept God's unconditional love. On another night at KAMC, Pastor Peter preaches that Christians should forgive others by relaying the story of how Jesus forgave Peter (one of Jesus' twelve disciples) even though Peter denied Jesus three times. Pastor Peter stresses that we should forgive, love, and place "restoration above revenge"—even if others "perform or act badly towards us."[6] In short, students are encouraged to "imitate Christ" in their lives.

Third, related to the above themes, various sermons emphasize the importance of spreading the gospel and evangelizing others. Students are taught to share their faith and talk about Jesus and his salvation to their families, roommates, co-workers, and other non-Christians. Many of the speakers do this by including one or more stories of missionaries in their sermons. At one of IVCF's weekly gatherings, a staff member talks about a woman missionary in Hong Kong who is "risking and sacrificing much" to spread God's words. After telling the story of the woman missionary and other apostles in the New Testament, he asks, "What are some ways that Jesus is calling you to be like these servants?"

Other times, the entire sermon focuses on the importance of evangelizing others. On a typical weeknight gathering, Jeff, the head staff of WU CCC, presents a sermon entitled "How to Be a Passionate Lover for the Lost." After sharing his childhood experience of feeling helpless when he lost his parents at an airport, Jeff asks us to think about our experience of getting lost. He then turns to the gospel of Luke and talks about how Jesus invited a lonely and lost tax collector, Levi, to leave his old sinful life and follow him. Levi was once lost but was found by Jesus and became one of his disciples. With this story, Jeff asks everyone, "Are you a passionate lover of the lost? . . . Do you want to be a catcher of men and impact others?" He then details the five characteristics of those with "a heart for the lost" and says that we should go out of our comfort zones and share the gospel with others. He further relays a story about a famous missionary who died preaching the gospel and asks everyone to make a list of friends who are not saved and pray for them.

In addition to the sermons, students give personal testimonies on how they met Jesus or revived their relationship with Jesus, and they talk about their past mission trips. On a weeknight at KCCC, Buyoung, the head of the praise band, talks about the struggles he had as an immigrant trying to figure out what to do with his educational and financial future. He then shares how a pastor helped him see that "Jesus is the one who is in control" over his life and will surely help him determine what to do with his life in America.

On another night at CCC, the leader of the praise band also gives his personal testimony. He talks about how he changed from a hedonistic rock star—who was heavily into drugs, women, and partying—to a follower of Christ. On the following night at KAMC, a student shares that he feared "not being good enough in the world" and that he looked good on the outside but was "totally dried up on the inside." This, however, changed when he personally met Jesus at a campus ministry retreat. On another night at KAMC, one of the student leaders, Peter, talks about how he "screwed up a lot" in his life—how he almost raped a girl and has problems with pornography. He then concludes that "you can come to Jesus even if you are not holy . . . you don't need to come to Christ after you are perfect."

Students also talk specifically about their mission trips. A CSF student leader shares how guilty he felt thinking about the new car he wanted to purchase when the kids at the Mexican orphanage that he visited were "in such need." He thus concludes that he does not want to "lead a materialistic self-centered life." On another evening, a female student relays how the beginning of her short-term mission trip to the Philippines was "miserable because it rained, the facilities were bad, and there were killer mosquitoes!" Later, however, she says that she prayed to God and received his help, which enabled her to share her testimony (of how she became a Christian) and be a source of spiritual encouragement to many.

As suggested in the above descriptions of sermons and testimonies, the delivery style of the sermons and testimonies are personal and informal. Pastors, staff, and students dress casually in khakis, T-shirts, and button-down shirts; they talk in a relaxed conversational tone and interweave personal stories into their sermons and testimonies. They do this as they encourage students to work on their personal relationship with God/Jesus, "imitate Christ," and witness to nonbelievers.

Programs and Activities

WELCOME AND ANNOUNCEMENTS

The six campus ministries at WU all follow the same basic format in their weekly services and offer similar activities and programs. As we have seen, most campus ministries start their worship services by singing praise for about thirty minutes to an hour. The praise is then closed with prayer, after which a student leader or staff member comes up to welcome everyone and give the announcements.

After almost an hour of praise, John, a senior at WU and president of KAMC, comes up to the front of the lecture hall. He enthusiastically welcomes everyone and talks about the various activities that KAMC has planned for the upcoming week—a special pizza dinner, a football game, prayer meetings—and reminds people to sign up for small-group Bible studies. He then introduces the speaker of the evening, Pastor Peter.

Across campus, another student named John, one of the student leaders of CCC, shouts excitedly, "Welcome to CCC!," and makes several announcements following the praise. John notes that there will be a dinner for the new freshmen and transfer students and reminds everyone about the upcoming "Surf Outreach" (co-sponsored by Athletes in Action, a national Christian fellowship for athletes). A perky blond woman then comes up to talk more about the Surf Outreach—how they will share God's words and take a survey at the outreach to find out what the "people believe about God and stuff." While the announcements are being made, various flyers and sign-up sheets for outreach and small Bible study groups are passed around the room.

At AACF, two students jointly greet the crowd and yell, "Praise the Lord!" The two leaders then introduce Eddie, who comes to the front of the room and talks about a "secular music fast." Instead of listening to secular music, he encourages everyone to listen to Christian music for a week. He then asks if anyone has any Christian CDs to lend out or is in need of them. If so, Eddie says that they should talk to him. The two leaders then come back up to the front and encourage everyone to invite their friends to a coffee/evangelizing event where they "can drink coffee and just talk about Jesus." Next, a student named Henry announces that there will be another "Sisters Appreciation Day" where the AACF "brothers" (the men) provide dinner and entertainment for the AACF "sisters" (the women).

At CSF, Josh, a senior at WU and the student president of CSF, stands in front of the room and welcomes all of the attendees, especially those who are new to the meeting, and asks everyone to greet one another. In response, people hug, pat each other on the back, smile, shake hands, and say "hi." Josh then announces an upcoming retreat where the CSF chapters will join together for "worship and fun" at a nearby conference site in the mountains.

KCCC's leaders speak in Korean, but their weekly gatherings follow the same format of welcome, announcements, and invitation to join various activities like the other campus ministries.

SKITS

A skit or special presentation commonly follows the sermon to either supplement it or promote an upcoming event in the campus ministry. On a weeknight after Pastor Peter finishes delivering his sermon at KAMC, several students who went to Mexico as short-term missionaries perform a mix of a hip-hop/ballet dance to a Spanish song to encourage students to witness to nonbelievers. On another evening at CSF, a man enacts nervously but successfully calling up a woman and inviting her to dinner at his apartment while three of his roommates cheer him on. The skit encourages students to attend a dinner where the brothers of CSF entertain and serve the CSF sisters dinner.

AACF also has skit presentations. On a Wednesday night, AACF's skit team, "Salt and Light," enacts students hugging one another after pretending to vigorously fight kung-fu style. The skit supplements the evening's sermon on the importance of loving one another, even one's enemies.

IVCF also has skits. On a Tuesday night, a multiracial skit team presents a skit mimicking a popular reality television show called "Survivor," where various people go through obstacles to win a million dollars. The difference between the skit and the show is that the winner of the skit overcomes multiple temptations like parties and the desire for extra sleep to receive "spiritual blessings" by coming to worship and hearing the word of God.

A skit at CCC on another night encourages students not only to come to the meetings but also to invite their friends to an evangelizing event. In the skit, a man pretends to lazily watch a football game on TV, while another man unsuccessfully tries to invite him to CCC's Surf Outreach. "So uh . . . like do you want to go to a surf talk? It's going to be cool; it will be so great, man. Do you want to go? Bryan Jennings (a famous surfer) will be there, that guy rules!" Absorbed in the football game, the man pays no mind to the invitation. The skit demonstrates what one should not do when inviting students to the Surf Outreach.

PRAYER, ANNOUNCEMENTS, AND CLOSURE

After the sermon or skit, there is usually prayer followed by final greetings and announcements. If new members were not welcomed at the start of the evening's program, they are greeted toward the end. At KAMC, newcomers are asked to stand up near the end of the worship; when they do, everyone claps. At CCC, the new members are asked to raise their hand; when they do, they receive Christian music CDs.

The final announcements usually remind students to take part in the various social and religious activities of the campus ministry. After the sermon, one of the student leaders of AACF asks everyone, "Did you guys have quiet time this week? If so, raise your hand." He then encourages students to secure private prayer time with God. Toward the end of CCC's weekly meeting, Bob, who is the leader of the "prayer team," reminds students about a collective fast that will take place and defines fasting as abstaining from food for spiritual purposes and "not because you want to diet . . . not for some political purpose." Another student leader comes up to remind everyone about an upcoming dinner for the freshmen and transfer students and jokes about how he loves to eat. At IVCF, students are encouraged to participate in a "God Investigation Group" and a discussion on race and faith. A special dinner for the black students at IVCF is also announced. At KCCC, there are even more religious and social activities, including a Christian sports and games gathering with other KCCC chapters near WU.

Overall, campus ministries' activities include: prayer meetings, praise team practices, leadership meetings, small-group Bible studies, weekend Bible retreats, community services, evangelizing "outreach" programs, sports and games, special lunches and dinners, school study sessions, trips to local amusement parks, and more. Students can be assured that they will find plenty of activities to occupy their time.

Following the final announcements and a closing prayer, the after-worship socializing begins. A loud buzz quickly fills the rooms as students discuss how their week went, how their classes are progressing, and what they are planning to do over the weekend. As the other attendees continue to socialize, student leaders eventually regroup to touch base on upcoming programs and organize future events. In some of the campus ministries, food is served after the service. At IVCF, there are donuts, cookies, and soda, and there is even a full dinner at KCCC. KAMC, CSF, AACF, and CCC do not serve food, but many go out for pizzas or burgers after the meeting.

Comparing Campus Ministries: Differences

SGKA campus ministries are the most distinct from the first-generation campus ministry, KCCC. Like AACF, IVCF, and CCC, the worship services of SGKA campus ministries are conducted all in English: the pastor and staff members preach in English, songs are sung in English, and all of their flyers are written in English. In contrast, the worship services of KCCC are conducted in Korean with a few English words sprinkled in: the sermons are in Korean, the participants use Bibles written in Korean, their posters and flyers are written in Korean, and the members informally speak to one another in Korean and use honorifics to refer to the older members of the group. These practices are evident in a typical KCCC weekly gathering.

Looking around the lecture room where KCCC meets weekly, one can spot several posters written in Korean that advertise the various events that KCCC holds. They include "summer missions," separate group meetings for "brothers" and "sisters," and sporting events. Many also bring Bibles that are written in both Korean and English or Bibles that are written entirely in Korean.

After everyone sings praise for about thirty minutes, one of the lead singers briefly prays in Korean. Then another one of the members who led the praise comes up and shares a "personal testimony," which is delivered all in Korean. Following the testimony, there is a video on "summer missions" sponsored by the CCC headquartered in South Korea, encouraging students to go on short-term mission journeys to foreign countries with other college students from Korea. After the video showing, Sung, the student president of KCCC, prays and introduces the evening's speaker, Pastor Kwon. While Pastor Kwon occasionally preaches in English, particularly if there are a few non-Korean-speaking students who are visiting, most of his sermons are delivered in Korean.

After Pastor Kwon delivers his sermon, KCCC members proceed with a group prayer where everyone simultaneously prays out loud. During prayer, some of the members shout, groan, or cry as if they are in deep anguish. While this kind of a loud and emotional prayer continues, a woman softly plays the piano. When she stops playing, everyone immediately stops praying.

This kind of group prayer, considered to be a distinctive "Korean-style" of prayer, is also conducted toward the end of both KAMC and CSF. The students at KAMC and CSF, however, do not pray as loudly as the members of KCCC, and some of the students at KAMC and CSF do not say anything at all as the others pray out loud. Moreover, KCCC regularly holds all-night prayer meetings at a large Korean church nearby. At these gatherings, students and staff from the various KCCC chapters near WU come together and pray from 10:30 P.M. to 3 A.M. KAMC and CSF do not have such intensive group prayer gatherings.

Compared with KAMC, CSF and the other three campus ministries, KCCC more personably and extensively welcomes new members. Toward the end of the official meeting, Sung asks the new members to come up to the front of the room and say "hello." When a few newcomers come up to the front, Sung asks them to state their names, year in school, and majors and to share something else about themselves. When this is done, all the members line up to shake each of the new members' hands and personally welcome them to KCCC. In addition to this welcome, the newcomers are asked to fill out a personal information page included in the flyer for new members. After the meeting, one of the KCCC leaders goes up to the new members and welcomes them once again and asks them questions to get to know them better. For example, they asked me how old I was, what church I attended, what I studied in college, and whether I had a boyfriend.

Following the welcome, there is a "group shout," fondly referred to as the "KCCC shout." The shout is exclaimed twice, first in Korean and then in English; it speaks about evangelizing the whole world. All of the students raise their right hand in the air as they shout. No other campus ministry had such an activity.

KCCC also stands out from KAMC and CSF because they commonly eat Korean food after the official meeting is over. At one gathering, the KCCC sisters prepared kimchi fried rice (kimchi is a spicy garlic-based vegetable salad that is *the* staple side dish in Korea). Other foods served after the weekly services include Korean *kim-bap* (Korean sushi) and *tuk-gook,* traditional Korean rice-cake soup.

As people eat and socialize, Korean is the language of choice. As is customary in Korea, older females are referred to as *un-nee* by younger women and *nu-na* by younger men; older males are referred to as *oh-ba* by younger women and *hyung* by younger men; the upperclassmen are referred to as *sun baes,* and the underclassmen are referred to as *hu-baes;* the pastor is called *mok san nim,* and the other Korean staff members are called *sun jang nim* by their religious titles. Many also quickly bowed to me when they found out that I was older than them, which did not occur in KAMC or CSF.[7]

There are thus various differences between the two SGKA campus ministries and KCCC. KAMC and CSF conduct all of their services in English. They do not read the Bible in Korean; their meeting hall is not decorated with Korean words. KAMC and CSF pray out loud like the members of KCCC, but the members of KCCC pray even louder, and some of their prayer gatherings extend past midnight. While the members of KAMC and CSF refer to their pastor or staff leaders by their first names, the KCCC members refer to their leaders by their religious titles; whereas the nonstudent leaders of KAMC and CSF are trained in American seminaries or campus ministries, the staff of KCCC are trained and supported by the CCC headquartered in Korea. KCCC also has a more extensive and personal welcome. And while many of the KAMC and CSF members go out to eat at fast-food restaurants near campus after the weekly worship service, KCCC members eat traditional Korean food.

Beyond the differences that one can observe between SGKA and first-generation campus ministries, SGKAs themselves note that they are the most unlike the first-generation campus ministries. They refer to the latter campus ministries as the fellowships for the "FOBs" (Fresh off the Boat; slang for recently arrived immigrants). An SGKA explains, "It is because they did not grow up here, they are FOBs. . . . I would have more to say to a white guy than [a first-generation Korean American] who is going to [want to speak] Korean and does not know much about American culture." Accordingly, SGKAs would more likely attend AACF, IVCF, or CCC than KCCC, particularly since many do not speak or read Korean well.

SGKA versus Other Non–Korean American Campus Ministries

As we have seen, SGKA worship services are not very distinct from the other three campus ministries. They all meet on campus, sing the same praise songs, study the same passages in the Bible, and have similar programs and activities. SGKA campus fellowships look much like any other Evangelical fellowship on campus. If anything, SGKA campus ministries are more advanced and innovative than the fellowships of their Evangelical peers.

Across the United States, Asian American groups, including Korean Americans, are pioneering a revival of a capella singing. On West Coast college campuses, Korean American Evangelicals are known for their cutting-edge praise music. Students of other ethnicities commonly note, "Oh, the Koreans have a great worship team." Indeed they do. Their praise music is very contemporary—they use the latest praise music coming out of the United Kingdom as well as the United States—often before the other campus ministries do the same. SGKA Evangelicals have also been praised by the larger Evangelical community for their zeal, growth, and mission work. They, along with other Asian Americans, have invigorated and enlivened the campus Christian community.

What, then, is really "Korean American" about SGKA campus ministries? What makes SGKA campus ministries stand apart from their non–Korean American counterparts? The differences can be grouped into variations in organizational structure, gender of the speakers, relationship between the younger and older students, welcome and outreach, and style of prayer. While these differences exist, they are not severe. And the variations may have more to do with the fact that SGKA campus ministries are smaller student-run campus ministries supported by local pastors than an inherited or distinct Korean culture. Within a diverse and competitive religious marketplace where Asian American Evangelicals predominate, what can be deemed "Korean American" and unique to SGKA campus ministries are also being picked up and adopted by the other campus ministries.

ORGANIZATIONAL STRUCTURE

One of the differences that first stands out about the two SGKA campus ministries is that they both have an elected president, vice-president, secretary, and two other student leaders that make up a core group of student leaders. While the other three non–Korean American campus ministries also have student leaders, they do not hold specific titles such as president, vice-president, and so on. Given that KCCC also has a president, and given that the first-generation Korean church is known for valuing titles and positions within the church, this type of organizational structure would seem to be something that the second generation inherited or carried over from the first generation. Further observation reveals that this is not entirely the case.

The emphasis that SGKA campus ministries place on these leadership positions may have more to do with the fact that both of the campus ministries are student-run campus ministries rather than an inherited culture. With relatively little support from paid or volunteer staff members, KAMC and CSF need to have a clear group of student leaders. Aside from the weekly sermons, the student leaders of KAMC and CSF are in charge of all other activities and programs within the campus ministry.

In contrast to KAMC and CSF, AACF, IVCF, KCCC, and CCC have several paid and volunteer staff members who play a significant part in the daily functioning of the campus ministries. As one of the larger national campus Evangelical organizations, AACF has four staff members who have been trained from the AACF headquarters to help run the campus ministry at WU; IVCF and CCC each have five staff members who have been trained by their respective headquarters to direct their campus ministries at WU. In contrast, both KAMC and CSF each have a nonstudent adult who oversees the campus ministries at WU. These nonstudent adult leaders function more as distant overseers and are not directly involved in the daily functioning of the campus ministry. Thus, having a clear set of four or five "core" leaders with particular designated functions is a necessity that comes from not having sufficient staff support as smaller, more localized campus ministries. Moreover, most other student-run organizations on campus have student leaders in the position of president, vice-president, secretary, and so on.

FEMALE SPEAKERS

Another notable difference between the Korean American campus ministries and AACF, IVCF, and CCC is that the Korean American campus ministries did not have any female speakers. The weekly sermons in the two SGKA campus ministries were always delivered by men, while AACF, IVCF, and CCC occasionally had female speakers. But this difference can not easily be attributed to a distinct patriarchal culture carried over from the first generation. It again has more to do with the fact that AACF, IVCF, and CCC are run mostly by hired or volunteer staff, while KAMC and CSF are for the most part student-run with the support of certified pastors who provide the weekly sermons.

There are very few ordained female pastors in the conservative Evangelical community. Accordingly, if IVCF and CCC had Evangelical pastors from the local community come and provide the weekly sermons like the Korean American campus ministries instead of their nonordained staff members, it is likely that they would not have any female speakers, either. Supporting this point, KCCC, which has more female than male staff members, occasionally has female speakers and is actually known for having strong female leadership. The gender difference in preaching may thus have less to do with traditional Korean culture and more to do with the organizational structure of SGKA campus ministries.

RELATIONSHIP BETWEEN YOUNGER AND OLDER STUDENTS

Another distinguishable feature of SGKA campus ministries is the close relationship between the upperclassmen and underclassmen. SGKAs do not use honorifics to refer to upperclassmen and underclassmen (*sun bae* and *hu bae*), nor do they make linguistic distinctions between older and younger students like the students at KCCC. Nevertheless, the upperclassmen in the SGKA campus ministries qualitatively function as the leaders, mentors, and older "brothers" and "sisters" for the underclassmen.

The juniors and seniors lead the freshmen and sophomore's small Bible study groups and help them with everything from spiritual matters to dating and relationships to giving advice on what classes they should take. A senior student at KAMC cooks for the freshmen in her small Bible study group every week and tries to make sure she knows "what is going on with each one of them." Another male senior of KAMC goes up to the dorms to eat with the freshmen students every week and plays basketball with them afterward. He says that this is his way of "reaching out to them and being there for them as an older brother." A freshman describes the relationship between the upperclassmen and underclassmen in this way: "The upperclassmen invite you, treat you, cook for you. . . . They want to get involved, share what they have learned and gained . . . like this is what college is about so that we can do the same thing later on." This kind of relationship between the older and younger students seems to reflect the traditional *sun bae* and *hu bae* relationships found in traditional Korean culture where the older students take care of the younger students and the younger students show deference to the older students.

Even if these relationships between the older and younger students reflect traditional Korean culture, such relationships are not unique to Korean Americans. Like KAMC and CSF, AACF, IVCF, and CCC treat the older students different from the younger students; the younger students (freshmen and sophomores) have separate small Bible study fellowships led by the older students or staff, and junior and senior students are often placed as the leaders, models, and mentors for the younger students. A white upperclassmen at CCC describes her role as a mentor and an upperclassmen: "As a mentor, as their sister [in Christ], I hang out with them, sometimes even help them do their errands because most of them don't have their own cars . . . and I cook for them too . . . not that often, but I try to become part of their lives, build relationships and try to be there for them."

These relationships exist in campus ministries because the older students are expected to act as the more mature Christian "brothers and sisters" who can mentor the new younger members of the campus ministry. When asked if the leaders of IVCF also pay for the freshmen when they go out to eat like they do in the Korean American campus ministries, a white male senior leader responds, "Yeah, we will pay for them too, but it is not because we have to, but because we want to serve them as brothers and sisters [in Christ]." Thus, it may be that the strong upperclassmen and underclassmen relationship in Korean American campus ministries has its roots in Korean culture. Nevertheless, this kind of relationship is not unique to Korean American campus ministries and can be found in other Evangelical Christian fellowships even if the extent to which it is found may vary.

In addition to the differences in organizational structure, gender of speakers, and relationships among students, SGKA campus ministries more actively welcome new members and practice a group style of prayer. These differences, however, can be minimized as campus ministries compete and interact with one another in a competitive and closely knit religious marketplace. In such a context, what may seem distinct about a particular campus ministry can be adopted by another campus ministry, particularly in a religious community where Asian Americans predominate.

WELCOME AND OUTREACH

One of the characteristics that make the Korean American campus ministries as well as AACF distinct from IVCF and CCC is their use of nametags and the extent of welcome that they have for the new members. Once one approaches the entrance of the lecture hall where KAMC meets, two female students can be found sitting behind a table smiling and welcoming the attendees and passing out name tags and a schedule of the evening's program. In front of the lecture hall where

CSF gathers, a male student can be spotted standing and greeting the attendees and passing out flyers that outline the evening's program. At AACF a young woman is seated behind a long table eagerly handing out name tags and the evening's schedule. On the table, there are various flyers advertising upcoming events like special dinners and sports games, along with pictures of AACF students taken from past social gatherings. An AACF directory that has the names, e-mail addresses, home addresses, telephone numbers, and birth dates of the members is also displayed on the table.

In contrast to the three Asian American campus ministries, no one stands or sits greeting the members of CCC or IVCF coming into the lecture halls to worship. IVCF has some flyers and informational pamphlets on upcoming events on a table near the entrance, but there is nobody behind the table. One can easily slip in and out of CCC and IVCF without being personally greeted by a welcoming committee or any of the other members. These differences, however, are not lasting.

When CCC leaders heard about several Asian American campus ministries handing out name tags and actively welcoming new members, they decided to do the same. When another predominately white campus ministry heard that the Asian American campus ministries were giving out free "back to school kits" along with their contact information to get the new students to join their campus ministry, they began providing free food and a raffle to give out Christian music CDs for the new visitors. Thus, what seems at one point unique to the Korean American or Asian American campus ministries can be adopted by the other campus ministries.

KOREAN STYLE OF PRAYER

Like other Evangelical campus fellowships, SGKA campus ministries have representatives pray for the group. But unlike other campus ministries, SGKA campus fellowships have group prayers where everyone simultaneously prays out loud.

Toward the end of the meeting, Pastor Peter of KAMC closes his eyes and bows his head. Seconds after, SGKAs do the same and join Pastor Peter in group prayer. Instead of having one person simply pray for the group to end the meeting like the other campus ministries, the entire congregation prays aloud and fills the room with a low buzzing sound. After everyone prays like this for about five minutes, Pastor Peter prays as a representative for the group. Toward the end of the weekly gatherings, CSF members gather in a big circle, hold hands, and also engage in verbal group prayer.

This kind of group prayer, referred to as *tong-song gi-do* in Korean, is viewed as the "Korean way" of praying and is commonly practiced in first-generation Korean churches and campus ministries.[8] This style of prayer, however, is not so foreign that other campus ministries are not willing to try it. For example, a Chinese American staff of a multiracial campus ministry who had experienced group prayer while visiting a Korean American friend's church came up to the front of the room after the weekly sermon, clapped her hands together excitedly, and said, "tonight, let's pray Korean style!" This meant that everyone would pray aloud at the same time. Thus, some non–Korean Americans actually find the "Korean" style of prayer desirable, or at least worth trying.

The members of the SGKA campus ministries also do not pray as loudly as do the members of the first-generation Korean American campus ministries. Some in the SGKA campus ministries murmur softly when they pray, or they do not pray out loud at all. Several SGKAs comment that they personally do not like to pray "Korean style." Moreover, other Christian groups (e.g., Pentecostals) pray out loud together as well. Thus, the so-called Korean style of prayer may not be so unique, and what can seem distinct to Korean American campus ministries can be adopted by the other campus ministries.

This kind of exchange and adaptability is facilitated by the fact that the religious marketplace at WU is vibrant, competitive, and closely connected.

Religious Marketplace: Competition and Incorporation

Particularly during the beginning of the school year, various campus Evangelical organizations set up their tables with bright signs on each side of a popular walkway at WU, trying to grab the attention of the thousands of students that pass through. Some step out of their booths and stand right in the middle of the walkway to pass out flyers and approach students walking by. One flyer for a campus ministry reads, "Come and enjoy the great food and fellowship!" Another Korean American campus ministry passes out their information on a miniature Chinese takeout box with their contact information written on the outside of the box. Inside the box, there is some candy and a heart-shaped eraser with a Bible verse attached.

Approaching one of the tables set up by the campus ministries, one can expect to be greeted with smiles and flyers and to be asked to fill out a contact information sheet to receive additional information regarding the group's activities. Some campus ministries provide special gift packages for those who sign up and provide their contact information. They offer free candy, CDs, drinks, and other "goodies" and are eager to tell students about their upcoming barbecues and other social gatherings. Passing by another table, someone shouts through the crowd, "Hey stop by, you might even find your future wife here!"

In a diverse and competitive religious market setting, religious consumers have a lot to consider; there are multiple campus ministries offering them various forms of religious goods and services. But religious consumers are not the only ones who are observing what is being proffered by the campus ministries. In a diverse marketplace, religious organizations themselves are carefully observing one another's recruiting and advertising practices. As they do this they often pick up on innovative ways of attracting and drawing more members and subsequently adopt them in their own campus ministries.

When the Christian student groups noticed the Hillel Jewish student organization singing to get the attention of students passing by, one of the Christian groups decided to bring out their guitars and sing as well. Meanwhile, another campus ministry decided to blast Christian rock music. When one campus ministry gave out free drinks, another decided to not only give out free drinks, but also free pizza.

This kind of exchange is encouraged by the fact that most of the major campus ministries are part of the Intercollegiate Christian Council (ICC). According to a former student president of ICC, ICC was formed to confront the "spirit of competition" among the various campus ministries and unite the campus Christian community and bring revival—to "strategize ways to bring Jesus Christ to campus." With this goal in mind, ICC holds several events throughout the school year to build community and evangelize the entire campus. In order to do this, student representatives from the various campus ministries, including KAMC, CSF, AACF, IVCF, and CCC, gather at least two or more times every month as part of the ICC.

At these gatherings, the representatives report on events in their own campus ministries and exchange ideas and thoughts on how to lead their campus ministries as part of a larger Christian coalition. The representatives then report back to their respective campus ministries on what was discussed and exchanged at the ICC meetings. The chance that the representatives of the campus ministries have to interact with the leaders of other campus ministries and exchange and share ideas provide opportunities for campus ministries to learn, innovate, and borrow ideas and ways of worshipping from one another.

Conclusion

SGKA campus ministries are a lot like other Evangelical campus ministries. Whether they are ethnic, pan-ethnic, multiracial, or predominately white, campus ministries all meet on a weeknight and work hard to draw new members. They sing the same "praise" songs, put on skits, and have similar social activities. As nondenominational Evangelical Christian groups, they share theological principles, hold conservative sociopolitical views, study common passages and themes in the Bible, and try to foster their faith and witness to nonbelievers.

Nevertheless, there are differences. SGKA campus ministries have distinctive leadership positions. There is a president, a vice-president, a secretary, and a few other "core" student leaders. SGKA campus ministries also do not have nonstudent female speakers. As we have seen, however, these differences may have more to do with the organizational setup of SGKA campus ministries than with a distinct Korean American culture. Unlike AACF, IVCF, and CCC, SGKA campus ministries are not supported by and are not part of a national campus Evangelical organization. They do not have paid and volunteer staff, and they function with the support of local ordained pastors. Consequently, they need a strong and distinctive group of student leaders and are unlikely to have ordained female speakers provide the weekly sermons.

Closer relationships among the older and younger students, the upper and underclassmen, and active welcoming of new members look like something that the SGKAs may have picked up from the first generation. But even if these relationships and style of welcome reflect traditional Korean culture or ways of relating that SGKAs adopted from the first-generation immigrant church, such relationships are not uncommon. Close relationships between upper- and underclassmen and active welcoming of new members are not unusual occurrences on college campuses.

Among the differences, the way SGKAs pray stands out the most.

While their prayer style is not as intense as the first generation's *tong-song gi-do,* SGKAs also simultaneously pray aloud as a group. It should be noted, however, that this kind of prayer is a contested practice by the first as well as the second generation and is found in more charismatic Evangelical congregations. Moreover, in a diverse and innovative religious marketplace, it may be a style of prayer that even some non–Korean Evangelicals find appealing.

Aside from their group prayer, however, SGKAs worship much like their non–Korean Evangelical counterparts. What, then, is the significance of the finding that SGKA campus ministries' worship services are really not so different? It is important because it tells us that SGKA Evangelicals are not turning to separate ethnic ministries because they have distinctive sermons, activities, programs, theology, praise, or even a unique style of prayer. As we will soon see, SGKAs are drawn to separate ethnic ministries because of the people. They go to separate ministries to be with other SGKAs, not because SGKA campus ministries offer a wholly different kind of worship.

4

Emergent Ethnic Group Formation

If SGKA campus ministries look so much like other Evangelical campus ministries, why are SGKAs flocking to separate ethnic ministries? The answer is simple: they want to be with other SGKAs. The substance of what binds SGKAs together and leads them to forge an emergent ethnic group identity, however, is more complicated. It involves three interactive micro and macro processes.

Preconditions: Search for Community and Opportunity

Search for Community

At the beginning of each school year, IVCF holds a special rally for new incoming students in a large ballroom. At one of these rallies, a former WU graduate who is now an IVCF staff member talks about finding her identity and community through "Jesus Christ" and the "fellowship" offered by IVCF. She begins by sharing that she did not want to be just another "nine-digit" number "lost in the crowd" and ends by sharing that she found herself and was "saved" when she "personally met Jesus" and became part of "the [IVCF] family."

This special rally is organized around the premise that freshmen come onto the campus scene searching for community. Campus ministries presume that students want to be known and connected—that they are seeking to be more than their social security, driver's license, and various other identification numbers and are looking for a genuine community of friends. They presume correctly. A senior reflects on what it was like for him to start college: "You are thrown into this new situation, which you have never been in before . . . which is really exciting, but also pretty scary, so you are looking for community."

This desire for community is especially strong in a large university like WU where the student population is in the tens of thousands and where it is difficult to establish close social relationships. A student describes WU in this way: "It is like this big . . . bureaucratic maze, and you are this rat running around. You really have to have your stuff together, or you will be lost." Another student explains how hard it is to make friends in such a setting:

> In classes you go there every other day or something and you see the same people, but you don't really meet them, you just kind of listen to your [teaching assistant]. People don't go out of their way to meet people. They don't really talk to each other. They might talk like "what did the professor say?" . . . but don't really interact with one another, . . . Maybe it is because [the school] is so big.

Yet another student relates how hard it is to make friends at WU: "Even if you make some friends in class, there is no guarantee that you will see those same people twice unless you make it a point to have classes with them again . . . unless you make a whole lot of effort." Thus, many students come onto the college campus searching for community but have difficulty finding it. In this predicament, campus ministries offer a solution. As previously noted, campus ministries are distinctively aware that students come to college seeking identity, friendship, and community.

When campus ministries note that they "seek out the lost," they do not merely mean those who are "spiritually" lost but those who are also "socially" lost. As a staff member of IVCF explains, "This is not just a place of worship, it is a place of community where you develop deep bonds with people." The students themselves are aware that campus ministries can offer a solution to their social dislocation, as one of them comments:

> The only way to get to really know people are through those groups . . . because in class you just listen to the lecture and leave, and most people just go back up to their dorms or to their apartments after class. They don't hang out all day in the same spot, so the only strong relationships that you can make are outside of class like in the various clubs.

Another student comments on why campus ministries are so popular:

Why are they so popular? It is a place to meet people, where you can expect to be treated with respect, it gives you a sense of family and belonging, community. . . . It is the fastest way to meet friends. You may meet one or two friends per quarter, but this way you meet way more people, and if you choose to join, you are automatically accepted.

In these "clubs," students meet regularly, share interests, and have the chance to make lasting friends. They can find friends to socialize, study, eat, and even room with. During midterm and final exam weeks, the older brothers and sisters in the campus ministry prepare special care packages for them. They have friends in campus ministries who will remember their birthdays and help them out if their car breaks down. They can also turn to fellow "brothers and sisters" in the campus ministry for advice on everything from relationships to how to pass a biochemistry exam. And what is more, all of these social benefits are offered free of charge. Unlike other campus organizations like fraternities and sororities, there are no financial costs to joining, and the campus ministries welcome anyone who is interested. As a student explains: "You don't need to rush and pay [money] to get friends, like you do in the sororities or fraternities." Anyone who is willing to join is technically welcome and can obtain the benefits of joining.

FINDING YOUR SIGNIFICANT OTHER: UNDERCOVER DATING

An important part of students' search for community includes a search for a "significant other," a boyfriend or a girlfriend. A student reflects:

People say that once you are out of college it is really hard to meet people, college is the best time to meet that special someone. . . . That is why by the time guys become juniors and seniors they start really looking around for a girlfriend. You are never going to have this chance to be with so many other single people again.

The search for a "significant other" during one's college years is a need that campus ministries can fill. Through the close friendships that are built within the campus ministry, one can find a boyfriend, girlfriend, or even a future marriage partner. These possibilities are communicated in what some students refer to as "undercover dating" within campus ministries.

As single college students, many are interested in finding that "special someone," a boyfriend or girlfriend. But as conservative Christians in a religious community that encourages "serious dating" or "dating with the intention of marriage," they need a careful and efficient way of finding a desirable mate without resorting to "random dating." Being part of a tight campus ministry community enables students to solve this sticky problem. In a close community setting, individuals can find out what the opposite sex is "really" like and get to know them well without ever dating them personally. A Korean American student from KAMC summarizes "undercover" dating in this way:

> It is ideal to find a significant other in [a campus ministry]. . . . If you are interested in a guy, most likely you will see him interacting, see how he is. It is better than one-on-one dating; it is more real. You always go out, hang out, we get to see how the opposite sex hangs out, and if you are still interested after seeing how they interact, then you can flirt when you go out as a group and go bowling, with a bunch of girls and guys. The guys will be like, "let's call apartment 301 because there are like five to six women there" and like people always ask each other, "Are you interested in anyone?" I tell you there is this huge undercover dating. They are all at that stage when they are looking, and it is better to interact in fellowship. You can see what the guy is like with others . . . how he interacts, what he is really like. It is really the best way.

Thus, students willing to commit to a campus ministry not only get a close family of friends, but a chance to find a significant other.

In these ways, being part of a campus ministry can offer the prospective member community, friendship, and even romantic love, but this does not detract from the religious functions of campus ministries. For those who are religious, a search for community also includes a search for fellow believers who can sustain their faith in an otherwise secular university setting. An SGKA senior puts it simply: "College is when you can break your faith, get lost in the crowd . . . so you have to meet good [Christian] friends."

RELIGIOUS SUPPORT: ACCOUNTABILITY

The importance of community and the role of campus ministries in helping individuals to sustain and even develop their faith during their tumultuous college years are clearly communicated in the term "accountability." Within the campus Evangelical community, accountability commonly describes the social relationships that help sustain and develop an individual's faith. Korean American as well as non–Korean American campus Evangelicals describe "accountability" and its function in these ways:

> Accountability is having solid friends . . . having guys that I can talk to that can be supportive of my faith, what I am going through.

> It is so good to find accountability, you meet fellow brothers that understand the same morals that you have so they are going to be there. . . . Others will say, "hey let's go drinking" and stuff . . . but with a Christian brother or sister, they will be like "Are you ok? Are you keeping up with your walk [with Jesus]?"

> Accountability is working with one another, supporting one another, following out what you believe in as a Christian together. It means I have other Christians keeping me in check, asking me questions, examining my life . . . to see if I am living in Christ. . . . An older person or partner keeps you in check and will be candid with you.

Many students talk about how obtaining this "accountability" with Christian friends was important to them, particularly given that they were in a new and secular college setting. A student reflects: "I wanted to join [a campus ministry] to have that accountability there because people warned me about going to college and how a lot of people fall away . . . so I wanted to have a group of close Christian friends." A freshman student looking for a campus ministry says: "I am looking for a place where I can grow, have discipleship, develop accountability, people I can go to for accountability. . . . It is important to have that especially during your college years with all these different things going on . . . also so that I can grow in knowledge of God's character." Another student elaborates how the strong relationships that he built with other Christians helped him sustain and even develop his religious faith during his college years:

> My biggest fear coming into college was that I was going to fall. I thought I would stop going to church because I had no ride, that things are going to go bad . . . that I would meet the wrong people. . . . I was

really worried about that. But God was really awesome. . . . Right when I came to school I met all these people in campus ministry and started hanging out with them more. And as the school year went on, I got closer to them. . . . When I look back at it, it was a real blessing. God was really looking after me. I did not want to fall, turn into a bad person, lose my faith, but ever since I stepped onto campus I've been growing and not going backward. I am really grateful for my campus fellowship . . . my brothers and sisters that keep me accountable.

Having this kind of accountability—strong social relationships with fellow believers—helps students in a variety of practical ways. "Accountability" is what prevented a Korean American male from going to a nonbelieving (non-Christian) woman's apartment when she called him late at night and "tempted" him to come over to her apartment. His "fellow brothers" from the campus ministry who lived with him told him to stay home and ignore the woman's call and avoid a potentially "sinful" encounter. Couples are also encouraged by other couples in the ministry to not "cross the line" and have premarital sex. A KAMC student leader dating another Korean American Christian explains:

If you have a boyfriend or girlfriend, get accountability, make sure someone knows that your private life is not something that you will handle yourself but you are going to give it over to God . . . not to what they think is right, but to God who established those standards clearly. So before you date, find someone you can be vulnerable to, really trust . . . open up to and admit, confess your sins. . . . not that he will absolve your sins, but that he will be able to point you to the one who can forgive you.

Another student talks specifically about how her roommates from the campus ministry keep her and her boyfriend "accountable": "We try to make sure that Jason and I are never alone in the apartment together and make sure that one of our roommates is in the apartment and leave the [bedroom] door open."

This kind of accountability is found in both Korean American and non–Korean American Evangelical campus ministries. The social relationships that are built through campus ministries help one to find meaningful friends and community. Many in campus ministries room together, play together, and study together; some later marry one another. They also help Evangelicals to maintain their faith during their trying college years. Thus, individuals come onto the college campus seeking community and belonging, and campus ministries are there to provide them just that.

Accordingly, students' desire for community—chance to meet friends, a significant other, and co-believers—draw them to campus ministries, including ethnic campus ministries. As we will soon see, however, this desire for community interacts with broader social structural factors. It interacts with structural opportunities for co-ethnic associations— namely, changes in ethnic density and diversity that make separate co-ethnic associations more possible.

Structural Opportunity: Changes in Ethnic Density and Diversity

For many students coming onto the WU campus, the large and impersonal setting of the university is not the only change to which they must adjust. They must also adapt to the fact that the university has a unique ethnic makeup; nearly 40 percent of the school population is Asian American (and nearly 10 percent of the school population is Korean American).[1] This kind of change in ethnic density simply offers Korean Americans and other Asian Americans seeking community more opportunities to build ethnic ties and participate in ethnic student groups, including those that are religious. One student's answer to why there are so many Asian American Evangelical organizations on campus, including Korean American Evangelical organizations, puts it simply: "Why? . . . because there are just so many of us!" Thus, changes in ethnic concentration afford Korean American students more opportunities to participate in Korean American and other Asian American campus ministries.

Related to changes in ethnic density are changes in the ethnic milieu of college and university campuses. As we have seen, higher education has become more open and receptive to ethnic diversity and explorations and expressions of ethnic identities. Ethnic student movements and ethnic studies programs inspired by the civil rights and black power movements of the 1960s helped lay the framework that altered colleges and universities to be more multicultural and sensitive to ethnic diversity. The Western European knowledge base of American higher education was contested, a tolerance of ethnic racial diversity became more accepted, and the pull of assimilation into the white core has declined. Matriculating into the major institutions of higher education can thus lead to heightened ethnic awareness and mobilization instead of greater acculturation and assimilation.

In sum, the search for community interacts with social structural opportunities—changes in ethnic density and diversity—to make separate ethnic associations, including ethnic religious organizations, simply more possible. In an ethnically dense and multicultural setting such as WU, individuals seeking friends, a significant other, and "fellowship" have more opportunities to congregate and associate with other co-ethnics.

Homophily and Ethnic and Racial Categorizations

Homophily

As a Korean American pastor notes, people want to worship and gather with those who are most like themselves: "In the Christian community we call it the homogenous principle . . . people want to worship with people who are like them."

Sociologists refer to this as *homophily*—the idea that "similarity breeds connection," that ties between similar individuals are more binding; more proverbially "birds of a feather flock together" (Duncan et al. 1972; Marsden 1987; McPherson et al. 2001: 415; Park and Burgess 1921). The same principle is at work in SGKAs' selection of religious organizations.

Given the opportunity to participate in a variety of campus ministries, those in search of community and belonging choose to associate with those who are most familiar and similar to them. For SGKAs, this means that they will associate with those who are most likely to share their experience of growing up in immigrant parents' homes and having intergenerational conflicts—straddling both Korean and American cultures.

FAMILIAR STRUGGLES AND FAMILIAL EXPERIENCES

In Bible studies, testimonials, and informal gatherings, SGKAs share stories about growing up in immigrant Korean families in America— struggling to please their parents, while trying to find their independent identity and negotiating between two cultures. A Korean American student describes the bicultural tension in this way: "At school you talk to your white friends . . . [with white friends], you go to sleepovers, paint your nails, eat pizza, but then you come home, you smell kimchi, and hear your parents speaking Korean, it is like a different world." Coming from such a background, being with other SGKAs who share the same bicultural and intergenerational struggles is more desirable than being with those who are less likely to share such experiences. As another Korean American student reflects: "Most of us have first-generation parents. We know what goes on in a Korean house . . . parents' pressure . . . 'study study study, marry a Korean, don't talk back.' So it is easier to get closer with other Koreans. They know where you are coming from. Even if you give someone the best explanation of Korean culture, it's not the same."

Among the shared familial experiences that Korean American students mention, pressures to excel in school are the most common, as an SGKA explains: "Korean parents are like you have to do this this this to be successful . . . you have to go to medical school or law school and study study study. They think the best colleges are Harvard, Yale, and Princeton. I am not saying white people don't stress education, but Koreans . . . they take it to another level." Another Korean American student relates that his mother wrote his personal essay and filled out a college application for Harvard University, even though he specifically told her that he did not want to apply: "My mom applied for me. She wrote my essays and everything . . . all grammatically incorrect. I even had to go to an interview. It lasted five minutes. I told her I didn't want to go there or apply, but she just wouldn't listen." The same student adds that he even knows of an SGKA named "Harvard."

Along these lines, Korean American students share stories about the pressures to please their parents by succeeding educationally and professionally, while also trying to develop their own independent identity. They explain that their parents consider a college degree in the social sciences to be a waste of time and money because they feel that such majors will not lead to financially lucrative careers. They pressure their children to major in business, engineering, medicine, or law—fields they believe will lead to a more financially successful and secure future. As a result, the struggle over choosing majors is a stormy battle between immigrant parents and their American-born and -raised children in the Korean immigrant family. For example, a student recalls how her brother severed his ties with his parents because they adamantly opposed his decision to be a cartoonist after graduating from Princeton. While extreme, this case illustrates the type and degree of intergenerational and cultural conflict that SGKAs face. SGKAs believe that fellow ethnics can best understand and relate to their experience of growing up in first-generation homes and having intergenerational and intercultural conflicts with the first generation in America.

Although their worship services are largely indistinguishable to other Evangelical campus ministries, Korean American campus ministries recognize that SGKAs share these experiences and attempt to be sensitive to their bicultural background and generational struggles. For example, an SGKA pastor states that white Evangelical organizations tend to focus on personal piety and offer a more individualistic form of Christianity and therefore cannot appreciate the social cultural background of Korean Americans. To illustrate this, he talks about how a white Evangelical campus ministry would not easily understand the tensions that Korean American students or other Asian students might experience when they want to "make a greater spiritual commitment" yet hesitate because they fear their parents' disapproval. Another leader of a Korean American campus ministry explains it in this way: "If a Korean American student had trouble making a decision to go to summer missions because her parents disapproved, we are likely to be more understanding and supportive of that . . . compared to, say, a white campus ministry." Thus, in comparison with white campus ministries, SGKA campus ministries can be *more understanding* of second-generation struggles and family ties and how it may influence their religious participation.

In addition to such sensitivity, being part of a Korean American campus ministry enables SGKAs to freely share various other experiences and aspects of growing up in Korean parents' homes in America. For example, being with other SGKAs means that they can use certain Korean phrases and share jokes unique to the experience of growing up in first-generation Korean homes in America. A leader of a Korean American campus ministry gives this example:

> Say like you are doing a joke on your dad . . . and like you are describing how your dad goes outside to wash his car in his dress socks with sandals with the *nan ning go* (a tank top that Korean males often wear) —that is funny to a Korean American because there is common understanding. . . . But with, let's say, a Caucasian . . . they wouldn't find it very funny.

An SGKA does not "need" to use certain Korean phrases and share particular jokes related to the ways he or she grew up in a Korean home in order to take part in a religious organization. But having the option to do so is nice.

The same applies to food. A Korean American student states that he would not be comfortable eating Korean food if he was in a "white fellowship." Although he eats more "American" food than Korean food, he says that being with other Korean Americans means that he would be more comfortable eating Korean food should he want to:

> I actually like kimchi, but when I hung out with mostly white friends, I would not eat it even if my mom served it because I did not want to stink. But with a group of just Koreans, you can eat it all you want. . . . It is okay if you stink because they will stink, too. It is not like I have to eat kimchi, but if I want to, it is not an issue [if I am with other Korean Americans].

SGKAs can take part in campus ministries without using certain Korean phrases and swapping jokes related to Korean culture. They can connect with other Christians without kimchi. Having these points of similarities, however, makes it easier.

WORSHIP: FAMILIAR PEOPLE

Many SGKAs not only grew up in immigrant parents' homes, they also grew up attending immigrant ethnic churches. As we have seen, SGKA Evangelical campus ministries look more like other mainstream campus ministries and were created in part as a reaction against what they disliked about the first generation's ethnic church. But what SGKAs do take away from their religious participation in first-generation churches is the experience of worshiping with other co-ethnics. Because their religious participation was experienced with other Koreans in the past, it is easier and "more comfortable," for them to continue to worship with other second-generation co-ethnics. Several SGKA students explain:

> It is not like I can't worship with, say, a black person next to me, but it is just what I am used to more. . . . Worship is a very private thing, and when you are used to it being with Koreans all the time, you kind of get set. . . . People are creatures of habit, so it is just more comfortable to worship with other Korean Americans. It is just what you are used to.

> Why did I pick a Korean one? It is not that I am racist. . . . I grew up with white people, but I don't know. I grew up in the Korean church and the majority of my Korean friends are Christian, while all of my white friends are Jewish. I never worshiped with white people, so I think that has a lot to do with it.

> I just felt like I did not fit in at the white church. . . . I had white friends before. . . . Maybe it is because church time is the time that I am used to being with Koreans, because that is what I grew up with. . . . It is what I am familiar with.

By seeking what is most familiar to them, SGKAs elect to continue worshiping with other co-ethnics.[2]

Given the choice, individuals seeking community and belonging will choose to associate themselves with those with whom they are *most* familiar—with whom they are likely to share the *most* similar experiences. It is not that SGKAs do not or cannot share intergenerational and intercultural conflicts and experiences growing up in immigrant parents' homes with other ethnic groups. But relative to other ethnic groups, they believe they share the most with other SGKAs.

As we will soon see, however, individual proclivity to turn to what is most familiar and similar at the primary group level interacts with ethnic and racial categorizations in the broader society.

Ethnic and Racial Categorizations

Our desire for what is familiar and similar interacts with ethnic and racial categorizations used by others in the larger society. Even if the SGKA in the following quote believes that she has the most in common with her white friends or any other ethnic group, imposed ethnic and racial categorizations by others make it difficult for her to be viewed and identified as such:

> When I was thirteen, I was with my girlfriends at a party at my friend's house and some of the guys were calling us, asking us who was at the party and my friend, Cathy (who is white) started naming off people. When she got to my name, I guess the guy on the other phone didn't know who I was, so in response Cathy said, "Oh, you know, the Chinese girl." . . . She was one of my closest friends, but she still called me the Chinese girl.

An adopted Korean American woman shares a similar experience:

> There are times when [my adopted white family] would be sitting at a
> restaurant or something, and people would just stare. . . . One time this
> kid at a restaurant stood up in the middle of dinner, pointed at me, and
> said something like 'look Mom, a Chinese girl.' . . . I can think that I am
> like my [white] sisters all I want, but others will not see me that way.

Another Korean American woman similarly reflects on her own experience of being racialized. "Growing up I never thought that I was that different. But I remember kids telling me, because they tend to be very
honest and direct . . . they would ask, 'Why is your face so flat? How can
you see from your eyes?'" Thus, even if one wants to be viewed as similar or like any other ethnic group, ethnic and racial distinctions used
by others in the broader society make it difficult for one to view oneself
as such. This is evident in the Evangelical campus community as well.

A Korean American student who went to the CCC weekly gathering
at WU recalls: "When I got there this guy told me, 'We are starting an
Asian thing that you can go to.'" This student was encouraged to go to
Epic, an Asian American CCC, even though he had come to take part in
the predominately white CCC simply because he "looked Asian." By
the same token, when Korean Americans pass out flyers to invite other
Korean Americans, they pass out flyers to those who "look Asian."
Thus, growing up in America as a Korean American means that one
will be categorized as a Korean or Asian no matter what ethnic group(s)
one may personally identify with.

In America, it is not just people on the street who use ethnic or racial
distinctions and categorizations. Various groups from the continent of
Asia are officially grouped as "Asians" by the U.S. government. The
census might gather specific information on particular ethnic groups,
but most data are aggregated as "Asian." Reports on the ethnic and
racial makeup of a college or university do not state what percentage of
Korean Americans or Chinese Americans are enrolled; rather, they state
that a certain percentage of the student population is "Asian." Asian
Americans are grouped by others in the larger society as being similar,
regardless of how they may group themselves.

The tendency to pursue what is most familiar and similar thus interacts with broader ethnic and racial categorizations in society to make
separate ethnic identifications and associations more likely. An SGKA

may think that he or she is "white" all she wants, but if others tell her and act like she is "Asian" or "Korean," it makes it hard to continue on with that belief. Indeed, much of our identity is shaped by how others view us. So if others keep telling us that we are not like them, it is difficult for us to continuously think that we are.

Desire for Majority Status and the Problem of Marginalization

Mobility and the Desire for Majority Status

As college students at top university campuses, SGKAs feel entitled to some benefits. They have worked hard, gained access to major universities, and entered into formerly white-dominant campus ministries. Being labeled by others and even themselves as the stereotypical model minority and now even the "moral minority" which seems to be reviving and leading the campus Evangelical community, they want the privileges attached to being successful and mobile:

> I am tired of being apologetic. . . . I mean I am at a top university, I am going to make over 100 Gs [$100,000 a year]. [I have] a hot car, a hot girlfriend . . . why should I be the minority and pander to whites? Why should I try to figure out what white people like? I am tired of "let's find a middle ground." . . . So I was like screw this, I am just going to do my own thing with my Korean crew.

As they strive to attain this, however, they find that they are not only categorized as being ethnically or racially distinct but are also marginalized as relatively inferior and have limited opportunities for mobility. They find that they lack relative power and access to resources that are available to the other ethnic groups, namely whites.

Marginalization

Several Korean American pastors and staff leaders point out that being in an ethnically or racially homogenous campus ministry means that Korean American and other Asian American students would have opportunities for leadership and growth, which they would not otherwise have in a diverse or white majority campus ministry. One of these leaders notes: "When I went to the headquarters [of one of the largest campus ministries in the U.S.] . . . do you know? It is still all white . . . no blacks at the top. . . . It is still white at the top. So if Asians want to move up in power, they can't do it over there."

Because it is "still white at the top," it is thought that Korean Americans and other Asian Americans can "grow the most" in an ethnically or racially homogenous organization that gives Korean and other Asian American students more opportunities for leadership. As an Asian American campus ministry staff explains: "We are separate because whites welcome Asians, but not into leadership positions, and they don't realize that by being status quo, they discriminate and make it hard for Asians to move up. . . . They are used to having leadership . . . so if Asians start their own separate organizations, they are more able to take on leadership positions." Being in an ethnically homogenous religious setting means that Korean Americans will have more opportunities for power and leadership. This is something that the older second-generation leaders and staff stress. But it is in the minds of the SGKA students as well.

SGKA students in their own separate ethnic campus ministries can escape any ethnic or racial marginalization that they may experience in the broader society as Korean or Asian Americans. As an SGKA student recounts, being in an ethnically homogenous Korean American campus ministry means that "you have the privilege of not thinking about the minority experience." Another student explains: "If you are with other Korean Americans, you are not going to be faulted for being Korean or looking Asian. You don't have to hear people say, 'Do you speak ching chong'? 'Do you guys eat dog?' 'Why are your eyes so small?'" Korean Americans do not have to "deal with" the negative stereotypes, prejudice, discrimination, and even simple misunderstandings that other ethnic and racial groups in the broader society might have about Koreans or those who "look Asian" if they are with other Korean Americans. Their ethnicity or race would not be an issue.

A Korean American student makes this point by sharing his experience at a white fraternity party: "I was at this frat party in the beginning of the year, just to check it out, you know . . . and no one was talking to me. Now, if I was a white guy I might think, 'Dude, what is wrong with me?' But if you are the only Asian guy . . . you are going to first think, 'Is it because I am Asian?' You are always going to have that thought in the back of your head." If he was in an ethnically homoge-nous setting like in a Korean American campus ministry, the issue of him being Korean American or "looking Asian" would not come up. He would not have to second-guess himself because of his ethnicity or race. Another Korean American student makes this comment by recall-ing his visit to Korea: "What I liked best about visiting Korea was that I felt this big burden, weight, lifted off my shoulders because I did not have to think about race, being Korean. . . . In America, a significant part of your energy in everyday life is exerted thinking about race. . . . You don't have to deal with that if you are just with Koreans."

A first-generation Korean pastor of an SGKA campus ministry fur-ther explains how Korean Americans or Asian Americans are racialized and are considered "strangers" and not "real" Americans in the larger society:

> To the first generation, the second generation say, "We are American" and act elite, but to whites . . . they are still strangers. Very few are just like whites . . . get into whites. . . . I am not talking about their profes-sional status, but talking about their heart and deeper level of con-sciousness. They are not white. Although Americans say they are multi-cultural, there are still differences [among] blacks, whites, Asians . . . you can't deny it.

Another Korean American student relays, "to [non-Asian Americans], we are all kung fu masters . . . perpetual foreigners." This is a reality that Korean Americans share with Chinese Americans and other Asian Americans, as one student puts it: "What unites Asians? . . . A lack of recognition from the rest of America . . . we are not included in the media. . . . Asian society is less popularly secure." Accordingly, some note that they grew up being warned that they will be racially discrimi-nated because they are labeled as Asians. A Korean American talks about how her parents told her that she has to work "extra hard" be-cause she is a racial minority—because she is going to be categorized as "Asian" in the larger society. Another Korean American shares that his father warned him that he has to be "better" than other applicants once he enters the "real working world," which he describes as dominated by whites: "We live in a predominately Caucasian society. Even if there are some successful Asians, they are very few. . . . So he was telling me that if there is a top job and an Asian and white are going for it, the white person is going to get it. So we have to be better to get the same job."

SGKAs who have strived and obtained socioeconomic mobility want to be treated accordingly; they want to have the status, power, and recognition in proportion to their achievement. Finding that these desires are not met in white-dominant or multiracial settings, they go elsewhere. They form and join campus ministries, organizations, where they can be the majority in power and not be marginalized as an ethnic or racial minority. Thus, individuals' desire for mobility and majority status interacts with continuing marginalization of ethnic and racial minorities to make separate ethnic religious organizations more desirable.

Conclusion

SGKA campus ministries are formed largely as a reaction against what the second generation disliked about the first generation's religious participation. SGKA Evangelicals embrace dominant white Evangelical practices and rituals, and their campus ministries look more like mainstream Evangelical campus ministries than either the immigrant church or immigrant campus ministries. This does not mean, however, that the second generation are assimilating.

SGKAs are not flocking to separate ethnic ministries because they have a uniquely ethnic worship style or distinct theology. Instead, they go to separate ethnic ministries for the people, to be with fellow SGKAs. There are three main interactive processes at work explaining what draws second-generation "Korean Americans" together and why they form and participate in separate ethnic campus ministries.

First, individual desire for belonging and community interacts with changes in ethnic density and diversity to make separate ethnic associations more possible. Second, individual propensity to cling to those who are *most* familiar and similar (homophily, or the "homogenous principle") interacts with imposed ethnic and racial categorizations in the broader society to strengthen ethnic group ties. Third, individual desire for majority status interacts with ethnic and racial marginalization to make separate ethnic associations more appealing.

Putting it together, SGKAs seeking religious community turn to ethnic campus ministries because changes in ethnic density and milieu on university and college campuses simply make it more possible for them to do so. Given that they are in an ethnically dense and diverse multi-cultural setting, SGKAs will seek out those who they are *most* familiar with—with whom they are most similar. This means that they will congregate with those who share experiences of growing up in immigrant families and churches and straddling two cultures. This tendency, along with the desire for majority group status and power, interacts with continuing ethnic/racial categorizations and marginalization to make separate ethnic associations more desirable. They are the basis of an emergent ethnic identity that is, in essence, "made in the U.S.A."

5

A Closer Look at the
Ties That Bind

It is "just *more* comfortable" was the most common response that SGKAs gave to why they were in separate ethnic ministries.
Indeed, having "comfort" is nice. It implies that one is free from sources
of pain, stress, and anxiety. It suggests peace of mind, warmth, security,
and ease. So what does it mean that ethnic ministries are simply "more"
comfortable compared with other ethnically diverse campus fellowships? A good way to look at this is to consider how SGKAs actually
compare themselves and relate to other ethnic groups in everyday life.
We can look at how SGKAs draw boundaries that converge as well as
diverge from two groups that they come into the most frequent contact
with within the campus Christian community—other Asian Americans
(specifically Chinese Americans) and whites.

SGKAs and Other Asian Americans

When SGKAs speak of other Asian Americans, they speak of East Asian
Americans. Out of East Asian Americans, SGKAs commonly compare
themselves to other second-generation Chinese Americans, with whom
they believe they share a contemporary immigration experience. Among
Asian Americans, SGKAs are also most likely to come into contact with
Chinese Americans within the campus Christian community.

Points of Convergence

CULTURAL FAMILIAL BACKGROUND

One of the similarities that SGKAs share with other Asian Americans, particularly other second-generation Chinese Americans, is their

cultural familial background—the experience of growing up in immigrant parent homes. They know what it is like to come from homes where English is not the first or only language with parents who are attached to the foods, cultures, traditions, and happenings of another country. Other second-generation Asian Americans know what it is to be bicultural and straddle two cultures. An SGKA student explains: "Growing up I was embarrassed of my mom because she could not speak English. She could not communicate with the white parents in my [cheerleading] squad. . . . With other Asians, there is more mutual understanding in that they know what it is like more because they come from immigrant families, too."

Second-generation Asian Americans have similar narratives of parents who gave up much to immigrate and give their children a "better life" and greater educational and occupational opportunities in America. An SGKA reflects: "We [Asians] are all immigrants in one form or another. Our parents gave up a lot to come [to the United States] . . . to give us a better life." Coming with such intentions, as we have seen, Korean and Chinese parents pressure their children to excel academically, attend prestigious universities, and settle into financially lucrative careers. As an SKGA shares: "What do Asians share? Common background . . . similar parents. . . . Every Asian parent tells me the same thing over and over again, 'Just study hard, make a good living.'" Another SGKA elaborates: "I think like the Chinese, like the Taiwanese, it is really hard for them to get into college [in their home country] like it is in Korea . . . so the parents immigrate to America to get their kids educated, so they really stress [education]."

Related to the pressure to excel, fellow Asian Americans share experiences of taking extra classes like SAT preparatory courses in the hopes of entering top universities. Once students take the SATs and enter college, becoming doctors or lawyers is considered to be most desirable. An SGKA male explains this reality by sharing how the parents of his Chinese American girlfriend pressured her into breaking up with him because he did not have a professional degree, specifically a medical or a law degree:

> She told her parents, "I have a boyfriend [who] graduated from Cal (UC Berkeley) [and is] making a good living as a computer consultant." What did they say? "No good." They want a doctor or lawyer; that is it. They said "That is it" and closed the door . . . typical Asian parents.

But white parents, they don't care about educational status like that. They just care about . . . "Is he a good man, does he treat her nice?"

Along these lines, SGKAs characterize Asian immigrant parents as more emotionally nonexpressive, strict, conservative, and controlling in their interactions with their children compared with the average white American parent. SGKAs explain that white children tend to grow up with "relaxed" parents who are more likely to be affectionate, treat their children as friends, and give them greater freedom and independence than Asian parents. As several SGKAs explain:

My [white] friends would say, "I love you" to their moms or dads every time they talk on the phone . . . like it came so naturally to them, whereas I don't even think that my dad has ever said that to me even once.

Basically with white families, you can talk to your dad or mom like they are your buddies. But in Korean families, you can't talk back to your father . . . you can't just say whatever you want to them. You are supposed to be quiet and listen to what they are saying even if you think it is ridiculous. It is different. It is not like the American families that you see on TV.

How [whites] are raised is different. When they are eighteen, they are out on their own, . . . but Asian parents . . . you are forever the child. . . . Like my friend Ken [a Chinese American], he is a junior in college, but his parents bought him a cell phone so that they can check up on him 24/7 [24 hours and 7 days a week].

Everything was more drama. . . . I remember my mom harassing me about wearing "hot pants" [tight short shorts], not being able to stay up late like my friends, date, party, go to sleepovers . . . just everything. Asian parents are [stricter] that way.

Of course, there are exceptions. There are certainly white parents who are strict, conservative, and controlling. But in the eyes of SGKAs, their parents and other Asian Americans' parents are more likely to share such traits than "the average white parent."

Coming from similar family backgrounds, Asian Americans share particular cultural characteristics, tastes, and preferences. As a result of being raised by immigrant Asian parents, SGKAs describe second-generation Asian Americans as generally quieter, less assertive, and more conservative than non-Asian Americans. A Japanese American staff member of CCC discusses this by explaining how Asian Americans communicate:

> I am not saying that it is like that for [every Asian], but there are just differences in interpersonal communication styles. [Asians] can't get a word in, different style of communication. Among Asian Americans, there is an etiquette of wanting to hear others . . . pausing, out of respect, but for many in a Caucasian environment it is very individual where it is up to you to get yourself heard.

This dynamic is also evident in multiracial settings.

In IVCF's conferences and discussions on "race" at WU, African American students were the most verbal in expressing their opinions and sharing their experiences in regard to race, followed by Latinos and whites. Asian Americans, for the most part, remained quiet. Noticing this, an Asian American IVCF staff member commented at the end of one of these gatherings that Asian Americans fulfilled the silent "model minority" stereotype by remaining quiet throughout the discussions on race. Along these lines, IVCF at WU has even changed the style of their small group Bible studies to be more accommodating to the growing numbers of Asian American students who were not as aggressive in sharing their feelings and actively taking part in the Bible study discussions.

At a broader level, some of the coordinators of student groups on college and university campuses observe that the atmosphere of their campuses has become more subdued with the increased presence of Asian American students. A religious organization coordinator who has worked at universities in the West Coast for thirty years explains: "With a sudden growth in the Asian student population, the campus changed. . . . It is not the radical campus that it once was in the '60s or '70s. The general feel is more conservative; there is less political activism, protest." A Chinese American graduate student who has been involved in several campus ministries shares this sentiment: "Stanford, Berkeley, and UCLA have become more subdued with more Asian students. . . . Haven't you noticed? The party atmosphere is gone, the air is more conservative. The fraternities and sororities are not as wild as they used to be."

Related to these characterizations, SGKAs point out that other Asian Americans are more likely to hold conservative values in dating relative to their non-Asian peers, as an SGKA student explains: "Dating and sex are less casual among Asian Americans . . . because in general I bet you anything that there is a world of difference between the ways an Asian American person was raised and how a Caucasian person is raised." Another student makes this point by noting that whites, relative to Asian Americans, would more likely think it "weird" that a teenager did not date in high school:

> Just the way you were raised is different . . . like dating. . . . Say I've never dated in high school and go to even a church group and was surrounded by Caucasians who have dated a lot in high school. . . . You go there, and so like that subject comes up [about not having dated in high school] in casual conversation, and they might think you are weird or the other way around.

Others comment that Asians have different gender expectations when dating, as a student explains: "It is just different. Say you date an Asian guy . . . you just know certain things. He is going to pay . . . he is going to pick you up, know what to do with your parents. With white guys, it is more up in the air."

There are SGKAs and Chinese Americans who are assertive, outgoing, and aggressive. Relative to other ethnic groups, however, as a whole, both of the groups are less likely to exhibit such characteristics.

Among the similarities that SGKA students say they have with other Asian Americans, the most frequently mentioned is food. As an SGKA student puts it simply: "What unites Asians? Rice!" Other shared foods and food ingredients include soy sauce, soybeans, fish sauce, hot bean paste, bean-curd, and sesame oil. SGKAs point out that there are foods that East Asian Americans are more familiar with, like ramen noodles, dumplings, and tempura, compared with other ethnic groups. Similar utensils, namely chopsticks, are also used by Asians. Asian Americans may only occasionally eat these foods and use chopsticks and some may not favor them at all, but they are more likely to be familiar with them than other ethnic groups in the broader society.

In addition to similarities in food, SGKAs share an emerging Asian American popular culture and its related consumer products. When asked how they are similar to other Asian Americans, SGKAs list various cultural products ranging from Boba tea (milk tea with tapioca balls) to specialized Asian style cars, commonly known on the West Coast as "Rice Rockets" (modified Japanese imports—Acuras, Hondas, Toyotas).[1] Other shared cultural products include Asian American magazines, Asian American literature, and Asian American films. There are also a host of websites that focus on Asian American consumer and cultural products ranging from Asian cartoons and music to jewelry. Along these lines, Asian American students at WU can eat sushi, drink Boba, read Asian American magazines, peruse the Asian American literature section at the bookstores, and watch Asian and Asian American films showing on campus or local theatres.

Furthermore, there are various "Asian hangouts" that SGKAs as well as other Asian Americans can share as part of the larger Asian subculture. Near WU, there is a street where various Asian foods are sold, with ethnic-specific as well as pan-Asian restaurants. There are Asian coffeehouses and teahouses that serve up trendy "Asian" drinks that service a mostly Asian clientele. There are video stores where one can rent Asian films, anime, and video games. Asian Americans can also find clubs and bars that Asian Americans frequent. The fact that other groups can take part in this subculture does not prevent Asian Americans from establishing a greater sense of shared identity and community through these cultural goods and businesses.

With increased concentrations of Asian Americans and access to symbolic and material Asian culture in and outside of the United States, today's Asian Americans have greater opportunities to express their identities as "Asians" in America. White and black symbolic and material cultures are not the only options. An SGKA describes this emergent Asian youth subculture in this way:

> Nowadays, the newest batch of Koreans knows what's up. They know what the deal is from the start. They already have Asians with them . . . they know how they are supposed to dress . . . not like going to [the beach] with white people trying to look like a surfer. Asians can [now] have their own sense of style and dress. . . . There are the dudes with the hot rice rockets . . . stepping up to real nice cars. . . . He is blasting Korean music like how black people play their rap music . . . playing it

real loud with attitude like you look at it and you say, "that dude has it together," and he has his hot Asian girl next to him with her makeup and hair.

Another student similarly describes the look of some Asian American men: "They have their hair slicked back or spiky on top and short on the side . . . They are not like going to be driving Ford Broncos. No, they are going to be driving fixed up Hondas and Preludes. They have their own thing going on." Other SGKAs note that one of the characteristics of the emerging Asian American subculture is an excessive focus on name brands: "Asians are crazy about name brands. . . . For example, if you go to a mall near where a lot of Asians live, you are going to see all of the big name brand stores. But I went to [a mall where there are a lot of blacks and Mexicans], they did not even have the Gap. . . . Now that's ghetto." In terms of music, Asian Americans within the growing Asian subculture generally identify more with hip-hop than alternative grunge type music, which tends to be more popular among white middle-class youth: "Asians, we are into hip-hop mixed with popular pop music . . . none of that grunge stuff, that gothic stuff, or country music . . . just like how Korean pop music is."

Thus, there are particular cars, hairstyles, music, and consumer tastes and preferences that SGKAs share with other Asian Americans as part of an emerging Asian subculture. Of course, not all Asians will identify with this subculture, and, even if they do, they will do so at varying levels.[2] Moreover, given the location of my field research, much of these cultural descriptions may be applicable to Asian Americans in the West Coast. Nevertheless, there is a growing material and symbolic Asian subculture, which Asian Americans can use to forge their group identity.

INTERACTIONS IN LARGER SOCIETY

Everyday interactions that SGKAs and other Asian Americans have with other groups in the broader society become yet another source of shared experiences: "Asian Americans get lumped and dumped together." Much of this has to do with the way Asian Americans look:

What do we share with Asians? Like in a room full of whites, Asians stick out. We are the only ones with black hair and black eyes . . . the only ones with a flatter face. You can't tell who is Chinese and Korean, but you can tell who is an Asian and who is not.

What unites us with other Asians? I think looks has a lot to do with it
. . . just that he has slanty eyes, too. People say "don't judge a book by
its cover," but people do it all the time.

With the physical lumping of Asians, there are various stereotypes and
prejudices that are directed toward some Asian Americans that affect all
Asian Americans. An SGKA woman relays how she has been called a
"chink," a racially derogatory term used for Chinese, although she is a
Korean American: "One time my family was walking around Second
Street, and a bunch of white guys in a truck stuck their heads out and
yelled, 'Go home, you chinks!'" Relatedly, Asian Americans, whether
one is a third-generation Japanese American or an SGKA, are commonly asked by other Americans, "Where are you *really* from?" and the
simple answer that one is from America never satisfies (Kibria 2002;
Okihiro 1994; Takagi 1993; Tuan 1998).

The tragedy of Vincent Chin, the trial of Wen Ho Lee, and the shooting of a Vietnamese student by Neo-Nazis, also hurt and threaten the
safety of all those who are viewed as "Asians."[3] A person who wants to
express his or her racism through physical violence to one particular
Asian group is unlikely to distinguish an individual as Chinese or Korean before assaulting them.

Along these lines, Asian Americans, particularly East Asian Americans, are commonly grouped together in America as the "model minority." Over a century ago, Asian Americans were categorized as stupid
and lazy. Since the 1960s, however, Asian Americans have been stereotyped as the smart and hard-working model minority.

In January 1966, William Petersen (who first coined the term) praised
the efforts of Japanese Americans in their successful attempt to enter
into the American mainstream in a *New York Times Magazine* article.
Peterson portrayed the Japanese as law-abiding, intelligent, and respect-
ful of authority. Later on in the same year, the *U.S. News and World
Report* also published a story praising Chinese Americans for overcom-
ing years of racial discrimination and achieving success (Osajima 1988).
Since the 1960s, this model minority image has been used to characterize Korean Americans as well.

The model image is not completely unfounded. Taken together, Asian
Americans fare much better than other racial minorities like African
Americans and Hispanics in major socioeconomic indicators, including

income, education, and occupation (Cheng and Yang 1996; U.S. Census 2000, 2002, 2003).[4] As recent scholarship has pointed out, however, the model minority image is exaggerated and problematic (Kibria 2002; Lee 1999; Osajima 1988; Takagi 1992; Woo 2000).

While the median family income of Asian families in the United States tends to be higher than that of whites, Asian Americans' personal income continues to lag behind. The median family income in 1999 for the total U.S. population was $50,046, and for Asian Americans it was $57,874. However, the per capita income for the overall U.S. population was $21,587 ($23,635 for whites) and $20,719 for Asian Americans (U.S. Census 2000).[5] In 2001, some 10 percent (1.3 million) of Asians and Pacific Islanders lived below the poverty level, compared with 8 percent(15.3 million) of non-Hispanic whites.[6]

The model minority image also obscures the fact that many Asian Americans overwork and do not achieve educational mobility in relation to their credentials (Woo 2000). Additionally, while Asian Americans are well-represented in professional occupations with their high levels of education and professional certificates, they are underrepresented in high-ranking executive administrative decision-making positions. They face a glass ceiling (Kibria 2002; Osajima 1988; Woo 2000).[7]

In recent years, the success of Asian Americans, whether or not it is overestimated, have also stirred anti-Asian sentiment and violence on college campuses and communities. MIT has become "Made in Taiwan," and UCLA has become "University of Caucasians living among Asians." Asian American students are represented as the nerds and resented as the "damned curve raisers," increasing the level of competition in classrooms and making the struggle for grades more difficult for everyone else (Nakanishi 1995; Takagi 1992).

This kind of resentment and fear of an "Asian invasion" at the major colleges and universities of America reflects an anti-Asian sentiment. In March 2001, white supremacist racist graffiti directed against Asians as well as African Americans and Arabs were found at Stanford. Examples of the anti-Asian graffiti include "rape all asian bitches and dump them," "white man rules," "nuke hiroshima," "kill all gooks," and "I'm a klansman."

With their high academic scores, Asian Americans are viewed as taking up too many of the desirable and scarce admission slots in prestigious colleges and universities. Like the Jewish applicants who encountered restrictive admission measures in Ivy Leagues, elite universities have been accused of using quotas to limit the enrollment of Asian American applicants (Nakanishi 1995; Takagi 1992).

This kind of "lumping and dumping" of Asian Americans can lead the different Asian ethnic groups to bond with one another as people on the "same side." An SGKA student who grew up in the Midwest with mostly whites talks about how comforting it was to occasionally spot another Asian face in a crowd: "When I was little, just seeing an Asian kid across the room, even if he was a boy and I didn't know him, that comforted me. I felt connected because we both [would know] what it was like to be a minority." Another SGKA comments: "Being Asians, I really believe that there is a sense of deep connection because we see each other as people that are on the same side." Interactions with other groups in the larger society then draw Asian Americans together. Given this, it is not surprising that Asian Americans identify themselves as "Asians" in addition to the more specific ethnic identities that they hold. SGKAs naturally and interchangeably use "Korean American" and "Asian American" or "Korean" and "Asian" to describe themselves.

Reacting in part to the shared disadvantages and hostility that they face in the broader society, Asian Americans also form various associations and coalitions. The growth of Asian American studies programs at universities are in large part an effort to fight the racism and oppression that Asian Americans as a group face in the United States. Asian American professional networks like the Asian American Bar Association and the Asian American Business Bureau try to assist Asian Americans by networking in a society that they perceive as somewhat hostile to Asians as a group. These organizations and associations can further strengthen the ties that specific Asian groups have with one another, making it more likely that SGKAs will find associations with fellow Asian Americans relatively "more comfortable" than those with other racial groups.

Points of Divergence

Second-generation Asian Americans share a cultural familial upbringing and get "lumped and dumped" together. But no doubt, there are points of divergences. Interestingly, these differences can be found within their similarities.

For example, martial arts are considered to be part of "Asian" culture, but each Asian country has its own form of martial arts: the Japanese have karate, the Chinese have kung fu, the Koreans have tae kwon do. In the same way, differences among Asian Americans can be found in the details of the similarities that they have. They are evident in Asian Americans' cultural familial background and experiences interacting with others in the larger society.

CULTURAL FAMILIAL BACKGROUND

SGKAs and second-generation Chinese Americans may have similar bicultural experiences growing up in immigrant parent homes, but SGKAs straddle Korean and American culture, not Chinese and American culture. The stories of immigrating to America from the old country are ones about Koreans moving to America, with ties and networks in Korea, not mainland China, Hong Kong, or Taiwan. SGKAs grew up exposed to two languages like other second-generation Chinese Americans, but SGKAs grew up hearing Korean, not Cantonese or Mandarin. Thus, certain phrases, terms, jokes, and names related to Korean culture cannot be understood by other Asian Americans. For example, a Chinese American student at KAMC (the only regular non–Korean American member) notes that he does not feel any difference between himself and his friends at KAMC except when he cannot understand certain jokes and phrases that SGKAs use. Even if they don't speak Korean well, SGKAs make particular jokes or comments using a few Korean words or references to Korean culture, which the Chinese American student cannot understand. Thus, behind the general similarities, there are differences in the details of what the two groups share.

Variations in food also demonstrate that what separates SGKAs from other Asian Americans are in the details. An SGKA previously noted that "rice" is the unifying food for Asians. But as an SGKA pastor elaborates: "Not all rice is the same." He states that he likes Korean rice the best because it is "sticky and moist," while the Chinese and Japanese favor rice that is more "separated and dry." As another SGKA explains: "Korean rice is different; it is moister and stuck together. . . . Chinese or Thai rice, my dad calls it 'flying rice'" because it is more separated and flaky.

The same applies for ramen noodles. Most Korean Americans and Chinese Americans from immigrant parent homes know what ramen noodles are and are likely to have eaten them, but the type of ramen that each of the two groups eat is different. Korean ramen is spicier and includes kimchi-flavored ramen—which is not commonly found in other Asian, like Chinese or Japanese, ramen noodles. Kimchi itself is a spicy fermented vegetable dish that is unique to Koreans, even though other nationalities have begun to consume it as well. Additionally, many Asian immigrants eat hot sauce, but their hot sauces are not all alike. An SGKA notes: "Korean hot paste, *go chu jang,* is more sweet and pasty, but Chinese or Vietnamese hot chili sauce . . . it is more liquidy and is not as sweet." Hence, the differences are again in the details.

These differences are not ground breaking. The fact that SGKAs may have grown up listening to Korean instead of Chinese, eating sticky rice versus flying rice, or even kimchi versus no kimchi is not going to determine whether one goes to heaven or hell. But they are the small points of similarities that constitute the ever illusive "comfort." They make SGKA Evangelical fellowships relatively "more" comfortable and familiar and therefore desirable than a Chinese American or a pan-ethnic Asian American campus ministry.

Other cultural traits set SGKAs apart from their Asian American peers. For example, SGKAs note that Korean Americans tend to follow what is known as "Korean time" and start their meetings and social gatherings later then scheduled; they enjoy "loitering" and "hanging out" for a significant period of time instead of quickly moving on to the next event. Relative to other Asian Americans, SGKAs believe that Korean Americans are the most "clicquey." SGKAs say that Korean American women are the "most exclusive," tending to date their own ethnicity more than other Asians like Chinese Americans.

Speaking of gendered relationships, SGKAs characterize Korean American men as more "aggressive," "authoritarian," and "manly" than other Asian American males. An SGKA communicates this by talking about the different characteristics of husbands and wives based on Asian ethnicity: "Out of Asians, Chinese American men make the best husbands. They are most likely to help you with the cooking and household chores . . . maybe it is the whole communism thing, I don't know. But, the Korean and Japanese men are supposed to be the worst. . . . And for men, Japanese women make the best wives; [they are] the most submissive and obedient." Whether or not these gender generalizations are valid, these sorts of group stereotypes are constructed and reconstructed by SGKAs to distinguish themselves from other Asian groups.

Growing up in Korean churches, SGKA Evangelicals also note that there are particular games that SKGAs play that are uniquely Korean.

They include various "clapping games," as well as games that embarrass people simply for the fun of it. Two SGKAs explain:

Only Korean people play fobby games like mafia, those sit-in-a-circle games like evolution . . . clapping and making animal noises.

In the games we play, the big thing is ridicule. It is cool in Korean Christian culture to make fun of each other, to do these embarrassing things like stick your head in a bowl of flour and search for Skittles, have people stuff as much marshmallows that they can in their mouths and say "chubby bunny," or bring up people that don't want to sing and make them sing.

These games are characteristically "Korean," which SGKAs, particularly those that grew up in the ethnic church, will be familiar with.

SGKAs further distinguish themselves from other Asian Americans by claiming that they are "the best" among all the Asians. Some SGKAs note that Korean men and women are the "best looking" and the "most stylish." Others insist that popular Korean culture is the "coolest" and the most developed among Asians. An SGKA shares: "It used to be the Japanese that led the Asian pop culture scene, but now it is the Koreans . . . Chinese, Japanese, Vietnamese, they all love Korean dramas [soap operas]. . . . Koreans rule!" Another SGKA expands on this point by talking about music: "You can rap in Korean, but not in Chinese; you can't rap in Chinese . . . the Chinese don't have the whole hip-hop culture down like the Koreans. . . . My Chinese friends they are all into Finkl [a popular Korean female pop band]. They have no idea what the heck [Finkl] are saying, but they love it. They don't have Chinese Finkl." These characterizations can be attributed more to in-group biases than to inherent differences between Koreans and other Asians; nevertheless, they can be used by SGKAs to distinguish themselves from other Asian Americans.

Within the broader Asian American consumer culture, there is also a growing Korean American consumer culture. There are Asian American magazines like *Yolk, Audrey,* and *Monolid,* but there are also separate magazines specifically for Korean Americans such as the *KoreAm Journal* and *Yisei Magazine.* There is also a growing literature on the broader Asian American experience, but there is literature that focuses only on the Korean American experience. There are Asian-themed restaurants and coffeehouses and teahouses that Asian Americans can frequent, but there are Korean-specific and Korean-owned restaurants, bars, clubs, and coffeehouses and teahouses that cater to Korean Americans.

Furthermore, with increased globalization, changes in technology, travel, and communication, Korean Americans can readily access music, art, movies, dramas, and other forms of entertainment in Korea for consumption in America. An SGKA pastor takes note of this by talking about an emerging Korean pop culture that is available for second-generation and even third-generation Korean Americans to consume in America—something that was not available for his generation:

> Back in my day being "Korean" was not really an option, but now these kids . . . they are clasping onto Korean pop culture, which really is a hybrid of American pop culture in the 1980s mixed with Korean culture. Now second- and third-generation Koreans in America are listening to Korean music, getting into this Korean pop culture and are dressing like Koreans in Korea. Now we have these [second- and third-generation Korean American] girls wanting to be typical Korean cuties.

Hence, beyond the broader Asian or Asian American culture, there is an emerging Korean American subculture that SGKAs can take part in and draw boundaries that distinguish them from other Asian Americans—that can make them more at ease with other SGKAs.

INTERACTIONS IN LARGER SOCIETY

SGKAs and the other East Asian Americans that SGKAs commonly refer to when they speak of Asian Americans share experiences being lumped together as "Asians," but they also have their distinct interactions and histories in America. Only the Japanese Americans have a history of internment linked to the bombing of Pearl Harbor and the hostility they faced from the rest of America during World War II. When Americans think of Pearl Harbor, they don't think Korean or Chinese, but Japanese and Japanese Americans. But when people think about the 1992 Los Angeles riots, they think mostly of Koreans, not other Asians. An SGKA makes this point by explaining blacks' interactions and attitudes toward Koreans: "Related to the whole LA riots . . . when black rappers sing about stingy liquor store owners, they talk about Koreans, not Chinese or other Asians. . . . In black films, you see them [criticizing] and shooting up Korean grocers, not Chinese, so I feel that blacks would have a more hostile attitude toward me [than toward other Asians]."

Additionally, Korean Americans note that they are not as well known in the larger U.S. society relative to Chinese Americans and Japanese Americans. Several SGKAs share that some people did not know who "Koreans" were when they were younger. An SGKA pastor comments, "I grew up being asked 'Are you Chinese or Japanese?' People really didn't know about Koreans back then. People didn't really know about Koreans until the '88 Olympics [in South Korea]." Another SGKA makes a similar point by commenting that most Americans are unfamiliar with Korean food and Korean restaurants relative to Chinese or Japanese food and restaurants. He notes, "Just the fact that whites are not as familiar with Korean food, whereas they are with Chinese and Japanese food, tells you how [Koreans] are not as popular. Wherever you go, you can find Chinese food, but not Korean food." Another SGKA comments: "Eating Chinese take-out [has become] like an American thing to do, but not Korean food."

In response to the lumping and the dumping that Asian Americans face in the larger society, various Asian American associations and professions continue to form. But, in addition to pan–Asian American associations, there are separate Korean American associations and coalitions. There are Korean American bar associations, Korean American university professors associations, and Korean student associations.[8]

A closer look at many of the pan–Asian American organizations also reveals that ethnic-specific ties remain strong. So-called Asian American associations do not commonly represent an equal share of the various Asian ethnic groups. Even within the campus Christian community, there are very few Asian American campus ministries that have a representative mix of Chinese, Korean, and other Asian groups. The Asian American Christian groups at WU tend to be either predominately Chinese American or Korean American. It is hard to find an equal mix of Chinese American and Korean American students in an Asian American campus ministry.

In sum, there are simply greater points of convergence among SGKAs relative to other Asian Americans. SGKAs and other second-generation Asian Americans tell similar stories of being caught in the middle and being marginalized. They can inhabit an emerging Asian American subculture and have similar group traits. But there are finer differences within these similarities that separate SGKAs from other Asian Americans—that make SGKAs feel more connected with one another. Thus, when given the choice, SGKAs turn to SGKA campus ministries where they can enjoy the maximum amount of homophily and comfort.

Korean Americans (Asian Americans) and Whites

When speaking about how Asian Americans are similar to one another, SGKAs speak in terms of how they are alike relative to whites. Whites are the major comparison group; African Americans and other ethnic minority groups are rarely mentioned. Relatedly, when SGKAs are asked to compare themselves to whites, they often do so by grouping themselves as Asian Americans.

Points of Convergence

CULTURAL FAMILIAL BACKGROUND

However defined, people across ethnic and racial lines grow up in families. Within families, there are fights between generations, tensions between spouses, conflicts among brothers and sisters, and divisions among relatives; but there are also bonds of love and affection whatever the ethnic and racial makeup of the family. There are happy and sad times, successes and failures, births and deaths, as everyone tries to figure out how to eat, drink, play, work, and die. Beyond these basic social human experiences, talking about how SGKAs and other Asian Americans are connected to whites invariably lead to discussions on what is "American" and the various cultural traits, tastes, and preferences that bind Americans together.

For many SGKAs, an "American" is a U.S. citizen who values the ideals of democracy, freedom, and individualism. An SGKA describes what he views as American: "When I think 'American,' I think of having the opportunities to pursue one's goals in a democratic free society. . . . It might not always play itself out like that, but the ideal is there. The American part also means that you have more individual freedom, less pressure to conform." Another SGKA explains how Americans value individualism relative to collectivism by taking note of differences in how Koreans versus Americans refer to themselves: "Americans say and write their own name followed by their family name, [whereas] the opposite is true for Koreans." In other words, someone who is called "Joe Park" in America will be referred to as "Park Joe" in Korea. Like the Koreans, the Chinese and the Japanese place their family name ahead of their own name.

In addition to enjoying democracy, freedom, and individuality, being American means one is part of a broader capitalist consumer culture, as an SGKA puts it: "We are all going to know about Britney Spears and Michael Jordan; . . . we all grew up watching the same [Saturday morning] cartoons." Another SGKA talks about sports: "How do I relate with whites? You can always rely on sports; . . . you can always talk about how [the Yankees] are doing and get a conversation going, you can't do that with an FOB." Immersed in the larger popular consumer culture, most young Americans know what singers are "cool," what styles are "in" and what places are "happening"; most grow up watching similar television shows, listening to the same top-twenty hits, and watching the same sports games. Even if Asian Americans may have additional pop subcultures in which they can traverse, they are connected to the larger popular culture through the radio, television, internet, videos, movies, news, and magazines that unite all Americans. An SGKA woman comments: "Just because you listen to Korean music and watch Korean dramas [Korean soap-operas] does not mean that you don't know about Jennifer Lopez and *The Young and the Restless.*"

Similarly, some SGKAs and Asian Americans may hang out at "Asian" clubs and restaurants, watch Asian films, play "Asian" games, and go to ethnic grocery stores. But they also go to Disneyland, McDonald's, and Starbucks. They shop at megamalls and "American" grocery stores and watch typical American blockbuster movies.

It is important to note that various ethnic subcultures interact and intermix with the broader popular culture. For example, the music that some SGKAs listen to, which they label as "Korean," is actually heavily influenced by American rap, hip-hop, and pop music. The same applies to movies and various other forms of entertainment that ethnic groups claim are authentic to them. By the same token, popular American culture is influenced by ethnic subcultures. Making this point, an SGKA explains how Asian films have influenced American films: "Movies like *the Matrix* and *Mission Impossible II* and *Charlie's Angels,* you can see the Asian influence in their fight scenes and in their overall style . . . and black people, white people, they all go to see it." Another student notes how Tae Bo, an aerobic kick-boxing workout that has gained popularity in America is "really a mix of tae kwon do [Korean martial arts] and American aerobics." Thus, the various ethnic subcultures in America also interact with the larger popular culture and influence one another, even as individuals continue to distinguish them as specifically ethnic or more mainstream. In the grand scheme of things, this kind of cultural fusion may capture what is in essence "American."

INTERACTIONS IN LARGER SOCIETY

As U.S. citizens, SGKAs live under the same political, educational, and economic systems with other Americans. They enjoy the same basic legal rights, privileges, and duties. They go through similar educational institutions and buy and sell in the same marketplace.

As Americans, SGKAs and other Asian Americans also follow various informal norms and mores with the rest of the hyphenated and nonhyphenated Americans. They learn how to function as customers, students, employees, drivers, pedestrians, and so on in the broader society. Everything from how one stands in the elevator to how one pays the waiter requires some form of basic knowledge about American culture, norms, and values. An SGKA explains, "There are just basic things that you know is American. Like when I went to Korea . . . you are not supposed to tip the waitresses, that is considered rude, . . . but in America, they might get psycho if you don't tip them 15 percent." Another comments, "Oh my gosh, in Korea you will see guys holding hands . . . and they have ultra feminine hair-dos. If you saw that in America, you would flip, you would totally think that they are gay." An SGKA also notes differences in everyday group interactions: "In Korea this *au-ja-shi* [Korean word for older man] bumped into me at the airport and nearly knocked me over, but he did not even say excuse me or sorry or anything. . . . [But being American], I was constantly saying 'excuse me' to everyone I was bumping into [at the subway, bus, crowded streets, etc.]." In these ways, whatever their ethnic heritage, Americans have certain values and norms of behavior that bind them together.

Points of Divergence

SGKAs most commonly refer to whites as the "other," the standard, the norm; whites are the major comparison group. As an SGKA explains, "You have to think . . . what is the defining mark, who are we different from? Whites, they are the standard." With whites being the majority, the "defining mark," Asian Americans are similar to the extent that they are different from whites. When asked how SGKAs are distinct from whites, SGKAs commonly speak of how Asian Americans in general are different from whites.

CULTURAL FAMILIAL BACKGROUND

The following comment by an SGKA is not entirely true: "Whites . . . they have just been here longer. They can say that their grandparents and their great grandparents were all in America, but we [Asians] can't say that." Chinese immigration dates back to the mid-1800s, and Korean immigration can be traced to the early 1900s. Overall, however, many Asian Americans, nearly half, are foreign-born (Logan et al. 2001). Picking up on this, SGKAs note that they and other Asian Americans are unlike whites because whites are less likely to share the experience of growing up in immigrant parents' homes and co-existing in two cultures.

Coming from immigrant homes with parents who are attached to the culture and ways of the "old" country, the look, feel, smell, and sounds of an Asian home are distinct from those in white homes. An SGKA explains: "My white friends wore shoes in the house, which I totally could not understand. . . . The way they eat is different. How? Koreans eat loudly, they slurp, slouch. There are no serving spoons . . . everyone just digs into the same food. . . . [Whites] think it is rude, but that is how Asians do it."

Relatedly, the way second-generation Asian Americans are raised by their parents is thought to be unique. As we have seen, Asian parents are generally characterized by SGKAs as more strict, conservative, authoritarian, and likely to exert greater pressures on their children to excel academically relative to white parents. An SGKA reflects: "My parents and I moved to New York, so I had many Jewish friends. . . . I went to so many bar mitzvahs. . . . But there is a difference in competitiveness [between whites and Asians] because [whites] are like third and fourth generation, so grades are not so important and whites do more extracurricular activities . . . not like Asians who just study." Even though these differences are generalizations and may not be entirely accurate, SGKAs believe that these shared cultural familial experiences separate them from the "average white person."

INTERACTIONS IN LARGER SOCIETY

SGKAs view whites as the "real Americans," and comparatively characterize themselves and other Asian Americans as "foreigners" and "aliens." Whites are portrayed as the group that has "true ownership" of America, while SGKAs and other Asian Americans have an uneasy second-class status. Many SGKAs share comments like, "When I think of an American, I think of the brown- or blond-haired and blue- or green-eyed white person. An Asian face does not come into the picture." Similarly, an SGKA recounts an experience he had when he traveled to northern California for the summer with his family: "We were at Tahoe, and this one white couple said, 'Hi . . . where are you guys from?' . . . and was like asking us if we knew how to speak English, saying it really slow. She just assumed that we were foreigners, like somehow we could not have been real Americans. She would not have done that if we looked white."

Another SGKA explains about whites: "Whites? They are not hyphenated. They are the consensus. They are more confident and free, more like this is their country." A white student who has participated in several of IVCF's sessions on "race" and racial reconciliation also comments on what it means to be white:

> What does it mean to be white? Not think about it . . . there are no ethnic studies for whites. White people are the ones who created racial classifications. You don't say "I am white." When you are the dominant group, you become invisible. Being white is not thinking about it. . . . I was always just "Hi, I am Phil," [I did not have to say,] "Korean American" when people ask, "What are you?"

As the dominant group, the norm, and the standard, whites differ from SGKAs and other Asian Americans in that they do not have the same minority experience. As an SGKA shares, "No one would question their presence in America and tell them to 'go home' . . . this is their home." In contrast to Asians who grew up as the minority group, whites have grown up as the majority with the accompanying privileges. Thus, whites are not as likely to understand the particular minority experiences of SGKAs like other Asian Americans. This reality makes SGKAs feel more connected and comfortable with other Asian Americans relative to whites. Accordingly, SGKAs would more likely take part in an

SGKA or another Asian American campus ministry than a predominately white campus ministry when given the choice to choose.

Conclusion

The overused phrase "it is just more comfortable" tells us that what really matters is the *extent* to which individual lived experiences converge and diverge. SGKAs are more comfortable in separate ethnic ministries because they want to associate with those who are *most* likely to share experiences growing up in immigrant parent homes, straddling two cultures, and interacting with others in the larger society as an ethnic or racial minority.

Experiences of marginality, in-betweenness, and being pressured to excel, however, are not unique to SGKAs. As my own study and other studies on Asian American identity show (Alumkal 2003; Jeung 2005; Kibria 2002; Lee and Zhou 2004; Min 1999, 2002; Tuan 1998), other Asian Americans inhabit similar realities. But what is key is that relative to other Asian Americans, SGKAs have more in common with each other. There are greater points of convergence.

With each other, SGKAs can complain about their Korean parents, crack jokes using certain Korean terms, and swap stories about what it was like growing up in Korean churches. As one SGKA puts it, "You don't have to explain certain basic things, cultural nuances, how our [Korean] families are, how we work, what we do that is hard to explain to others." They can take things for granted and feel a greater sense of ease with fellow SGKAs.

Accordingly, when given the structural opportunity to choose between a pan-Asian versus an ethnic-specific SGKA fellowship, SGKAs choose the latter. Compared with whites and other racial groups, however, SGKAs would choose pan-Asian fellowships because the points of convergences are greater and the divergences fewer. Seeking what is more or most comfortable thus means that individuals will go where they can be with those who are *most* likely to have similar familial and cultural backgrounds and experiences interacting with others in a setting where ethnic and racial "lumping and dumping" persist.

6

White Flight and Crossing Boundaries

A student in the IVCF at WU talks about a white family friend, Bob, and his experience searching for a campus ministry at UC Berkeley: "Bob's parents wanted him to get hooked up with a campus ministry and were concerned that he had not yet done so. When Bob's family asked him why he did not [join a Christian campus fellowship], he said that 'all of the fellowships are mostly Asian' and that he did not feel comfortable in any one of them." In the end, Bob joined a Christian fraternity instead of a campus ministry. Bob is not alone.

When Asian Americans start becoming the numerical majority in a campus ministry, white students take flight. They turn to other campus ministries that remain predominately white or drop out of campus ministries altogether. Accordingly, SGKA and other Asian American Evangelicals' separate ethnic religious participation cannot be understood without considering how their Evangelical peers respond to their growing presence. If students like Bob stayed in campus ministries that have witnessed a growth in the number of Asian American students, there would be more multiracial campus ministries. Instead of staying, however, most leave.

The same three interactive factors that make separate ethnic campus ministries the most desirable for SGKAs also make separation desirable for whites. The only difference is that whites have the power, are used to having it, and intend to maintain it, while the ethnic minorities do not yet have it and want to obtain it. In short, whites flee and forge their own ethnic ministries and emergent ethnicity for essentially the same reasons as ethnic minorities.

Why They Leave

Preconditions: Search for Community and Opportunity

White students want community and belonging like any of the other students stepping onto a large university campus. They want to be more than a statistic; they want friends, significant other(s), and a "family away from family." For Christian students, there is also a search for a fellowship of like-minded believers. In this situation, white students at WU find themselves in an ethnically diverse school setting where Asian Americans make up almost 40 percent of the population. While there are many Asian Americans, however, there are many whites as well; whites also make up nearly 40 percent of the student population. Thus, structural opportunities to establish close contacts with other ethnic groups exist, but opportunities to establish close ties with other white Americans remain.

One of the ways that white students can satisfy their desire for community is by joining fraternities and sororities, many of which remain predominately white. In fact, it is suspected that the fraternities and sororities on campus have witnessed a boost in membership in conjunction with the growth of Asian American campus ministries. A WU campus pastor reflects: "A lot of white students who feel lost with so many of the Asian campus groups around are turning to traditional student organizations like fraternities [and sororities]." A WU student also adds: "Where do the white students go? They go where they will find other whites . . . the fraternities and sororities. . . . I bet that their enrollment increased because white students don't feel comfortable joining the Asian campus ministries. If you want to find the white students, you should study the sororities and the fraternities." A Korean American student from CSF similarly comments: "The one place you are guaranteed to find a lot of whites are at the fraternities and sororities. . . . The party scenes, . . . they are still primarily white." White Christian students in search of community thus have the option to turn to these traditional student organizations, including Christian fraternities and sororities. But they also have the option to turn to campus Evangelical organizations that remain predominately white or have been newly created to attract white students.

On the WU campus, there are two large predominately white campus ministries—Christian Evangelical Students (CES)[1] and Campus Crusade for Christ (CCC). Supported by one of the affluent local churches near campus, CES began as a mostly white campus ministry and remains as such with about 200 members. The other white campus ministry, CCC, became a predominately white campus ministry after a separate Asian American campus ministry within CCC, Epic, was created.

Both CES and CCC do not advertise or refer to themselves as distinctively "white" campus ministries. Nevertheless, they garner white students and are unofficially known around campus as the two main white campus ministries. One of the student leaders of CES explains how white students find their way to her group: "We don't recruit and say we are mostly white . . . [the white students] just come, just by word of mouth. They seem to know what we are about beforehand." Informal social ties and information channels seem to lead white students to her campus group, even though they do not actively recruit white students.

Like CES, CCC also gets white students without advertising that they are a white campus ministry; but they also get white students by directly recruiting students in the fraternities and sororities, which continue to be predominately white. As the head staff of the predominately white CCC notes, "We had some Bible studies for the sororities and fraternities because we wanted to explore what it would be like to be more welcoming to white students." Accordingly, white students in search of campus ministries have options.

Homophily and Ethnic and Racial Categorizations

"ETHNIC MINORITIES WANT HOMOPHILY"

Part of why white students have these options is because mainstream campus Evangelical organizations presegregate their organization and presort the ethnic minority groups into separate ethnic ministries. Assuming that ethnic minority students want to worship with other co-ethnics, large campus Evangelical organizations like CCC create ethnic ministries for the different minority groups (e.g., Asian Americans, African Americans, and Latin Americans). From the perspective of Asian American and the non–Asian American staff in CCC, minority students would be served best in separate "contextualized" ministries of their own. They thus create separate ethnic ministries for them.

Intentional or not, constructing these separate ethnic ministries for the major ethnic minority groups also means that white students can have their own unofficially white campus ministry without having to directly make a case for it. At WU, CCC was able to create a white CCC by simply separating out the largest racial minority group on campus, Asian Americans. By creating a separate ministry for Asian Americans, "Epic," the main CCC on the WU campus was able to revert back to what it was, a predominately white campus ministry. Accordingly, whites are not simply "pushed out" of campus ministries that have become increasingly more Asian American. By presorting ethnic minority students into separate ethnic campus ministries, whites indirectly form their own campus ministries; they construct their own reactive and emergent sense of groupness.

This kind of presegregation and group boundary construction is done by emphasizing the desire of ethnic minority groups for what is most similar and familiar, particularly in terms of their cultural familial upbringing. One of the Asian American staff members of Epic describes why CCC started a separate ministry for Asian Americans:

> We now see quite a lot of Asian Americans, but over time we saw that they were not very comfortable with the ministry . . . because CCC was predominately Caucasian and so even after they receive Christ and start to grow, many of them ended up switching to another ministry like AACF [Asian American Christian Fellowship], where they felt more comfortable. So CCC saw a need that if they want to truly reach all students, they should create an environment where different types of students would feel comfortable. . . . So part of Epic's desire is to create an environment where we can deal with specifically Asian American issues . . . in an environment where they would not have to stop being Asian American to be a part of it. . . . Because I think in the past in a predominately Caucasian environment . . . often many Asian American students . . . for them to fit into the very white CCC, they would have to function very white and would not have much of a voice in the ministry. And often the ministry did not understand their culture like family pressures, issues of shame, . . . different uniqueness and obstacles Asian Americans had in their spiritual growth and in just their maturity.

From this staff member's explanation, we can see that ethnic campus ministries like Epic are created so that Asian Americans can be in a more "comfortable" cultural environment. Focusing on East Asian Americans who make up the majority of Asian American Evangelicals, Epic is a place where Asian Americans can be themselves—where

"Asian American issues" can be addressed. Epic would be sensitive to family pressures and "issues of shame" and other different unique cultural familial traits that distinguish East Asian Americans from others. The head staff of Epic talks more about what East Asian Americans have in common:

> We have thus far focused more on East Asians, and we recognize that there are some general themes . . . including a high relational viewpoint, a focus on family relationships. There is a high value on family coming out of a filial pride background, and there will be more of a shame-based relationship. They are also coming out of immigrant cultures or having an immigrant experience, even as second or third generations, that make them unique.

Another Asian American staff member of Epic explains what brings East Asian Americans together and why Epic was started: "Asians tend to think that if we just work hard enough, we will be recognized, whereas non-Asian cultures don't think that way. . . . They are going to speak up. Asians are not willing to be proactive. So in a contextualized setting like Epic, they can have more of a voice." Accordingly, it is argued that East Asian Americans share strong family ties, experiences of immigration, and particular ways of relating to one another that make them "more comfortable" in a contextualized Asian American campus ministry.

By providing Asian Americans (the most sizable Evangelical Christian population among the ethnic minorities at WU) this kind of a separate campus ministry of their own, the remaining CCC can unofficially be the "white" campus ministry. By letting Asian Americans have what they want, white CCC students get what they want as well. They can have their own campus ministry without having to make a case for creating a separate white or "European American" CCC.

"WHITES WANT HOMOPHILY TOO"

Although the case is not made by campus ministries that white students also want what is most familiar and similar, their desire for homophily is evident in their interactions with and reactions to the different ethnic groups. A white sixth-year "super senior" who did not leave when his previously white campus ministry eventually became 80 percent Asian American explains why he stayed when many of his white peers did not:

There is the issue of white flight. It is not something that has ever been an issue for me because I grew up in a diverse range of cultures. I actually went to the Westminster Vietnamese English-speaking youth group with my [Vietnamese] friends, so being with Asians is comfortable for me. It is what I was used to. But as for why the other whites don't stay . . . I would say they just feel uncomfortable with it. They aren't used to being with so many Asians . . . like it is not the campus ministry they knew before when it wasn't so Asian.

Because he grew up familiar with Asian Americans and diverse cultures, he was not uncomfortable with the demographic shift that took place in his campus ministry. But since most whites did not grow up like him, they leave when Asian Americans become the numerical majority.

Formerly white campus ministries are not the only campus ministries that have witnessed white flight; multiracial campus ministries have experienced it as well. Although IVCF is a diverse campus ministry that accurately reflects the ethnic demographic of the larger WU campus, several of their white students left when they made changes to accommodate other ethnic students. In an effort to make their campus ministry more multicultural and welcoming to an ethnically diverse student body, IVCF began singing some of their praise songs in Spanish. They also had an African American woman lead their praise band. When these changes were implemented, however, several white students left IVCF. They left to join the predominately white CCC. One of the IVCF staff members recalls:

Some of the white students left when we had a more African American gospel style of doing praise. . . . Once the black students led, the style changed and as you noticed we also sang songs in Spanish, some of the white students just did not like it. They desire to worship in the way that is comfortable to them. They just weren't used to that style . . . many of these students went to CCC.

Once the number of ethnic minority students significantly increases within a campus ministry, white students must make a choice. They must either adapt and meet the needs of the different ethnic groups or leave and search for a campus ministry or another comparable organization where they will not have to make such adjustments. Faced with this choice, few stay.

Thus, while white students' desire for what is familiar and similar is not made explicit by CCC leadership or the white students themselves, their desire for homophily also explains why campus ministries are pre-segregated. It explains why Asian American and other ethnic minority students are channeled into separate campus ministries and why emergent ethnic identities are constructed on both sides of the divide.

Ethnic and Racial Categorizations

To pursue homophily and presegregate campus ministries, broader ethnic and racial categorizations are continuously applied. An Asian American student who happens to stop by one of the unofficially white CCC meetings may be redirected to Epic. This kind of rerouting using ethnic and racial categorizations is often achieved even before students get a chance to find their way to the predominately white CCC.

A student leader of CCC describes what CCC does when they get a "response card" (a personal information card that CCC gives out to students on campus) from an Asian American student indicating an interest in joining CCC: "If we get a card from an Asian, we would usually give it to Epic. . . . If there was no Epic, [the white CCC] would just keep it, but otherwise we would give the card to Epic." Thus, a student showing interest in CCC will routinely get redirected to Epic, the Asian American CCC. Epic also actively recruits and passes out flyers and approaches students who "look Asian." And some of the staff of Epic are planning to recruit potential members from the Asian fraternities and sororities.[2] In these ways, Asian American students are categorized as distinct and routed or rerouted to the Asian American CCC even before they have the opportunity to participate in the unofficially white CCC. These efforts enable white students at CCC to remain largely undisturbed by the surge of Asian American students.

Desire for Majority Status and the Threat of Marginalization

Whites are used to being the majority and want to remain as such. As the number of ethnic minorities increases, however, they find that their majority status is challenged. As ethnic minorities, particularly Asian Americans, become the numerical majority and demand equal access to power and resources within the organization, whites who are accustomed to having unquestioned majority power and status feel threatened. In a multicultural university setting where diversity and equal rights are championed, however, they cannot just tell the ethnic minority students to go away. Accordingly, white students leave. They leave in search of a campus ministry or another comparable organization where they can enjoy their own homophily and maintain their majority group status without contest. One of the staff members of IVCF has this to say about "white flight":

> If a campus ministry tries to empower one group, say Asians, then the other group like the whites feels disempowered and fall away. . . . It is even the same with gender . . . when the [IVCF] leadership became more female, when women became more empowered in the organization, the male population dwindled. As the women got empowered, the men left. The same applies to the racial dynamic of the group.

Thus, the desire to remain as the majority then explains why whites "fall away" in a multicultural context where overt racist attempts to segregate and exclude ethnic and racial minority groups are not accepted.

Whites' desire to maintain power and majority leadership positions is also used to explain why Asian Americans separate, as an Asian American campus ministry staff explains: "We are separate because whites welcome Asians, but not into leadership positions." An SGKA student leader also comments: "Whites are used to having the power, so they would naturally feel threatened with so many Asians coming in." A Chinese American director of IVCF similarly notes, "Whites ask why don't you [Asian Americans] come to our [white] church but don't ask why they don't come to our [Asian American] church. . . . That is the majority mentality, that we should adapt to them, not them to us."

As white students want to maintain their majority status, however, they find that not only are they fast becoming the numerical minority but also they face the threat of being marginalized and categorized as the "other," the stranger. This is evident in several white students' comments regarding why they did not join a formerly white campus ministry that is now predominately Asian American. A white student explains:

> As a white person, I feel threatened. . . . In the beginning . . . because I was not the majority, it was so weird. I was too scared, how do I approach them? It is hard to go up to [Asian Americans]. I definitely feel threatened. If I went to an all-Asian campus ministry, I would feel like I

am invading them, and they will look at me and be like, "What are you doing here?"

This student felt uneasy, "weird," not being the majority and assumed that she would not be welcomed in an Asian American majority campus ministry. Another white student comments: "I came to WU and went to check out campus ministries, but I was always the only white person there . . . and I felt like everyone looked at me like I didn't belong. I felt alienated." Feeling out of place as the only white person in the "mostly Asian" campus ministries, this student decided to join a white sorority instead. A white student who is involved in a white campus ministry as well as the Associated Student Union also describes what it is like to be "white" at WU:

> There is racism on campus, and it is not by whites but by minority groups. . . . I knew this one girl, she wanted to go in and run for the office of president, one [minority] student told her, "Oh you are white, you can't run." . . . Then there was this white girl who was more Chinese than anyone else and wanted to run for the president of the Chinese Student Association, and she was booed off stage saying: "You are not Chinese!" The WU community is racialized where if you are white you can't do anything . . . being white is a handicap.

Used to being the majority, white students not only feel like "strangers" in an increasingly diverse multicultural setting, they believe that they are even being marginalized. Thus, part of the reason why white flight occurs is because white students, who expect to continuously be the majority in power, do not want to negotiate their power status and compromise their position as the majority. Turning to the remaining white-dominant student organizations or creating separate unofficially white organizations enables them to maintain their majority status without contest. It means that they can enjoy their own homophily undisturbed.

Crossing Boundaries

We have seen how individuals segregate when given the choice to integrate at the primary group level. This, however, does not mean that ethnic boundaries cannot be crossed. They can and are being crossed. But crossing them is relatively more difficult, costly, and unlikely.

Given the choice, most Korean Americans participate in Korean American campus ministries, but some do participate in predominately white campus ministries.[3] The stories of the Korean American students who participate in white-dominant campus ministries suggest that "assimilation" into the traditional white middle class at the primary group level, although difficult, is possible. One of the two Korean Americans who participated in the white Christian groups in college grew up with mostly white friends and did not have any social ties to the local Korean churches near WU. However, she grew up in a Korean home, attended a Korean church, and speaks fluent Korean. When asked what makes her different from the other Korean Americans who participate in ethnic campus ministries, she responds:

> The most popular people in my school were always white, so I tried to attach myself to that and for the most part, I was successful: I had a white boyfriend, I was in the cheerleading squad. It may not be as easy as being with just Koreans . . . but why limit yourself? I remember one of the white girls in my squad telling me that I was pretty for an Asian girl. That got me mad . . . like I was in a different category, but so what? I can do everything she does and do it better. It may be hard, but you can assimilate.

Another SGKA student who was once the youth group president of a Korean church explains why he is different—why he is now in a white church and continues to have mostly white friends:

> I don't know, maybe it is just my character. . . . I don't get easily stressed out . . . like in a job interview, the [white] guy interviewing me asked me if I would want to be in foreign relations versus working in a firm in America. . . . Maybe another Korean would think he is being prejudiced . . . but I understood why he would think that: I am Asian, I speak Korean, so maybe I would want to go overseas. I don't get mad because he assumed that. Mainstream society is open. You can assimilate if you want to. In fact, I think Koreans should assimilate. . . . I mean, what did they come to America for?

This student is more optimistic about the prospects of assimilating into the traditional white majority group and felt that doing so is desirable.

From his perspective, associating exclusively with other Korean Americans or Asian Americans in a Korean American campus ministry would itself be marginalizing. He explains, "I actually think it is marginalizing to be with just Koreans . . . it would be boring . . . it would just accentuate the fact that you are inferior and can't compete in the bigger pond." Convinced that he can compete in the "bigger pond" with the dominant group (whites), he consciously chooses friends and organizations that take him outside of the Korean American and the Asian American circle; he is part of a white fraternity and dates white women.

Korean American students who distinctively make the effort to "assimilate" even though they have the option to congregate with other co-ethnics suggest that boundaries can be crossed. And their decision indirectly implies that those who do are somehow more competitive, resilient, and challenging. This is evident in how some SGKAs in separate ethnic campus ministries view other Korean Americans in predominately white campus ministries:

> I would think that [Korean Americans in white campus ministries] would be more out-going, more confident . . . which I would associate with whites.

> Maybe they have a more positive attitude. They are more ambitious with a stronger sense of identity.

> They are not satisfied being the president of the Korean Christian club, they have more of a challenging spirit.

The idea that those who participate in white campus ministries would be more ambitious, challenging, and competitive is also evident in what some of the Korean American students say about why many Korean Americans would stay within their own ethnic circle: "If Koreans are with other Koreans they are bolder, but not when they are with white people because you have confidence when you are with your own circle." Other Korean Americans make this point by talking about interracial dating, as a Korean American man points out: "Everyone likes white girls because they are tall and pretty . . . like the really pretty ones are white. But as Asian guys, we don't have a chance. You rarely see Asian guys with white girls. . . . Pretty white girls are with white guys who are like 6'3. . . . So it is just more comfortable with Korean girls." According to this student, Korean American men turn to Korean American women because they cannot adequately compete with white men to get the more attractive white women. These comments indicate that the Korean Americans who participate in white campus ministries may be more confident, challenging, and ambitious; they are willing to compete in the "bigger pond" with the white majority even if it may be more difficult.

Others, however, have a less favorable view. A pastor of an Asian American church characterizes Asian Americans who socialize exclusively with whites in this way: "Who would go to [the mostly white] CCC? . . . Those who have self hatred, who want to be the white middle- or upper-class, those who reject their ethnicity." Others describe these Asian Americans as "white-washed," "sell-outs," and those who are in "self-denial" about their true ethnic identity. An SGKA male student elaborates:

> They are the sell-outs, the bananas, the Korean haters. They are ashamed of who they really are. . . . I mean if those Korean girls only want to date white guys, isn't that like a self-put down . . . like I don't like my own self? If they want some guy with blue eyes and blond hair . . . isn't that hating who they really are? It is self-hatred.

A Korean American student who formerly associated only with whites explains why he now has mostly Korean and Asian American friends:

> I just got tired of trying to blend in. I was tired of being the loner trying to drive a [Ford] bronco . . . going to Catalina with white people, trying to be a surfer. I was tired of being embarrassed about being Kim [having the last name "Kim"], because I look Korean with a Korean [last] name. . . . Now I am like, look, I am going to be proud of it. . . . I am tired of figuring out what white girls want, I know what Korean girls want. . . . With Asian girls, attraction is simple . . . they see certain cues, symbols. . . . You know what is going on, but with white girls, I don't know.

Compared to associating with whites, being with fellow Korean Americans is easier; it requires less effort and causes less social psychological stress. Another SGKA who associated mostly with whites but now has primarily Korean American and other Asian American friends and describes herself as a "born-again Asian" shares a similar story:

> I thought being white was the best, I would want to look white, be white. I deliberately tried not to hang out with Asian people, not date them, not get into the Korean thing, because I was programmed to think that it was inferior, but after a while I realized, [whites] are not for me, so why should I be for them? Why should I try hard to be what I am not naturally? I still talk to some of my white friends, but it is harder to have those relationships last.

Whether Korean Americans in white campus ministries are "more ambitious and challenging" or simply "self-haters" in denial of their true identity (or both) is difficult to say. It is also likely that those who cross ethnic group boundaries later bounce back and form co-ethnic ties.[4] But what is certain is that ethnic group boundaries can be crossed at the primary group level, even if crossing may not be the easiest or, for some, the most desirable path.

In an ethnically diverse and multicultural setting, whites can also cross group boundaries and have primary ties with other ethnic groups. Two of the Asian American campus ministries that I visited each had a white man who regularly attended their weekly services. One of these two white men, Ron, is in many ways more "Korean" than other SGKAs. Ron loves to eat Korean food, speaks Korean fluently, studies Korean history in East Asian studies (as a graduate student), and is married to an SGKA woman. Most of Ron's friends are Korean American, and he attends a predominately Korean American church. The participants of the Asian American campus ministry that Ron attends often praise Ron for being "very Korean" or "more Korean" than other SGKAs; Ron is applauded for being able to eat spicy kimchi and for speaking, writing, and reading Korean better than most SGKAs.

In the case of the other white man in the larger Chinese American–based Asian American campus ministry, most of the members did not know why or how the white man came to join their ministry. But some suspect that he may have a penchant for "Asian culture" and "all things Asian." A female student explains, "He strikes me as one of those guys with 'Asian fever' and 'Asian fetish' . . . being all into Asian girls and all things Asian." Her friend adds, "He always sits in the back and checks out the Asian girls, I think he has a thing for Asians." The student in question is a graduate student who was originally brought in by one of the staff members who is also a graduate student.

From the responses of Asian American students, the few white students who willingly join a predominately Korean American or Asian American campus ministry are stereotyped in two main ways. At best, they are viewed as sophisticated, open-minded white Americans who are willing to traverse different cultures and adapt to the norms and cultures of another ethnic group. At worst, they are stereotyped as deviants with a "fetish" and a penchant for the "exotic."

In sum, ethnic group boundaries can be crossed. A Korean American can participate in a predominately white campus ministry, and a white American can participate in a predominately Korean or Asian American campus ministry. Integration at the primary group level is possible. Intimate close ties can be established with other ethnic groups. But going against homophily and the broader ethnic and racial categorizations, facing the prospect of being treated as the minority is undesirable. Accordingly, crossing ethnic group boundaries at the primary group level is possible but relatively unlikely when the choice to maintain separate co-ethnic ties is available.

Conclusion

In this chapter, we examined how SGKAs' separate ethnic religious participation is shaped by their interaction with other ethnic groups, namely whites. We looked at why "white flight" takes place and how mainstream campus ministries racially presegregate their organizations and construct their own sense of groupness. Results ultimately show that the same three factors that make separate ethnic campus ministries a desirable option for SGKAs make separation desirable for whites and help them construct a reactive emergent ethnicity of their own.

White students want community, too. And in an ethnically diverse setting where there is a sizable white population, whites have the opportunity to form and join mostly white associations. Given this precondition, separate ethnic associations are desirable because white students also want homophily. They want to pursue what is most familiar and similar to them and be with those who are similarly categorized as belonging together. They want to run their campus ministry in the way that is most comfortable for them, in the way that they are used to, and not have their dominant position be challenged by the surge of ethnic minorities. Thus, whites form and congregate in separate white associations for essentially the same reasons that make ethnic minorities separate. The only difference is that whites are used to having the majority group status and want to maintain it, while ethnic minority groups do not yet have it and want to obtain it.

An important part of my finding on ethnic group formation is that one of the ways that whites strengthen their group boundaries and form white campus ministries is by simply giving ethnic minorities what they want, separate ethnic ministries. Campus ministry leaders recognize that white students may feel estranged with so many Asian American Evangelicals crowding the religious marketplace. As the head staff member of CCC recalls, "We were sitting behind our desks on [the popular walkway on WU where most of the other campus ministries set up their tables], and we noticed that everyone [from the other campus ministries] was Asian, . . . so we saw a need for a campus ministry where white students would feel more welcome." Realizing this, however, leaders of campus ministries in the contemporary multicultural university setting cannot just tell the new ethnic minorities to stop coming so they can keep their fellowship predominately white. They also cannot just come out and say that a separate "European American" campus ministry needs to be created. So the leaders of the large national Evangelical campus organizations take a more subtle approach. By forming ethnic ministries and separating out the large ethnic and racial minority groups, white campus ministries can be indirectly created.

With the creation of a separate ethnic ministry for Asian Americans, Epic, the original CCC at WU was able to revert back to a mostly white campus ministry. The main CCC at WU became a white campus fellowship without ever having to make an explicit case or justification for creating a white or European American campus ministry. By simply moving the Asian American students out, CCC became mostly white. Thus, Epic was created so that Asian American students could have their own separate contextualized fellowship. But it was also created so that white students who feel lost with the emergence of so many Asian American Evangelicals can have their own ministry as well.

For their part, ethnic minorities are willing to have separate ethnic ministries created for them, or they create their own by themselves. They would rather separate than directly challenge and confront whites' desire for homophily and majority group power within a single organizational context. Recognizing that whites want to run their campus ministry in the way that is most familiar and comfortable for them and maintain their hegemony, ethnic minorities retreat into their own organizations without actively engaging in a power struggle. Whites are thus not simply pushed out of their organization, and separate ethnic ministries are not created solely for the sake of ethnic minorities.

Overall, this shows us that it is precisely at the point of primary group contact that ethnic boundaries are drawn along both sides of the divide. Ethnic minorities are not willing to settle for a subordinate group status, and whites are not willing to yield; whites do not want to compromise their majority group status and homophily and adjust to the needs and preferences of the growing number of ethnic minority groups. In other words, ethnic minorities are not willing to be involved in the kind of traditional assimilation where assimilation is simply "done to them"—where they are the only ones changing, adapting, and shedding their differences in the process of incorporation. And whites are not willing to engage in the more contemporary and egalitarian view of assimilation where they, too, change and adjust as the new ethnic and racial minority groups assimilate at the intimate primary group level. Thus, separation goes both ways, and the construction of emergent ethnic identities is not unique to any single group.

While separation is the preferred path at the point of primary group interaction, ethnic group boundaries at the intimate primary group level can and are being crossed. A white student can participate in an SGKA campus ministry, and an SGKA can take part in a predominately white campus ministry. Additionally, there are multiracial campus ministries that try to meet the needs of multiple racial groups and check and balance the different groups' power relations. But crossing racial boundaries is relatively more difficult and carries additional costs. One will have to go against homophily and ethnic and racial categorizations, bear the cost of being a minority, and risk being marginalized. Accordingly, separation, rather than integration, remains the norm, and emergent ethnic identities continue to be constructed by the minority and majority alike.

7

"Why Can't Christians All Just Get Along?"

Evangelical scholars and leaders are becoming convinced that multiracial churches are "biblical" and that monoracial churches fall short of the mark as "true Christian churches." In their recent study on multiracial congregations, Curtiss DeYoung and his colleagues (2003) conclude that "all churches should be multiracial" if they want to heed Jesus Christ's call for inclusive worship—that his church be a "house of prayer for all nations" (Mark 11:18). Along these lines, a Christian is defined as a follower of Christ whose essential "way of life is racial reconciliation" (DeYoung et al. 2005: 35).

Indeed, the Bible's teaching that "there is neither Jew nor Greek . . . for you are all one in Christ Jesus" (Galatians 3:28) and that the gospel must be "preached to all nations" (Mark 13:10) conflicts with the reality of segregation in the church. The fact that over 90 percent of America's Christian churches are racially segregated—far more than most secular educational and government institutions—is an embarrassment according to many Evangelicals (DeYoung et al. 2003; Emerson and Smith 2000). SGKAs agree.

As an SGKA notes, it seems wrong that SGKAs are taking part in ethnically separate fellowships when "heaven isn't segregated"—when Jesus preached an essentially inclusive gospel message: "It's not like there is going to be a Korean section in heaven, . . . so I don't think it is right for us to all have our own separate thing."

Christians should be united by Christ, not ethnicity. Jesus was all about breaking down boundaries, not putting them up. This goal points to the broader tension between ethnic separatism and religious universalism. On the one hand, Christians want to worship within separate ethnic enclaves. On the other hand, however, their faith preaches an inclusive message that transcends ethnic and racial boundaries. SGKAs in separate ethnic ministries are thus conflicted.

The Tension

A black student started attending the weekly worship services of Korean American Mission for Christ (KAMC). But after three meetings he stopped coming. Two white men walked into one of the Christian Student Fellowship's (CSF) weekly gatherings after hearing the praise music from the outside. After ten minutes, they walked out. These incidences trouble SGKAs.[1]

SGKA Evangelicals say that they feel a moral guilt over the possible ethnocentrism of their religious practice. They wonder if they are not living up to the "Evangelical" and "Christian" name by having their own separate ethnic religious organization. As an SGKA explains, "It is kind of a shame if we can't go beyond our little circle. I don't even have any Christian friends who are not Korean, so it is like, what the heck am I doing?" Another reflects, "You have to think . . . what would Jesus do? He is not going to let ethnicity or race divide people. He was all about breaking down barriers, not putting them up." Other SGKAs point to specific passages in the Bible when they speak about this tension:

> I was reading the Bible and you know . . . back then there were all of these different ethnic and racial groups, too, but Apostle Paul said in Galatians about how there is now "no longer Jew or Gentile for we are now all one in Christ." . . . The Jews and Gentiles really had a hard time getting along, they had deep cultural differences. For example, even just in eating together—do we eat meat or not? They were major issues, but Paul was like . . . it is more important that we be together than separate. Why? Because Christ died for us all! So if it is possible to get Jews and Gentiles together, then it is more than enough to get Koreans and Hispanics [and other ethnic groups] together.

For these reasons, when a white or black student occasionally comes knocking at their door, SGKAs are conflicted. They face moral guilt and normative ambiguity. They wonder if they should stay ethnically exclusive and pursue what is relatively more comfortable or forego maximum comfort and worship with the greater Christian body.

This dilemma is heightened when SGKA Evangelicals think of how "nonbelievers" may perceive their separate Korean American Christian groups, as an SGKA shares: "We were all talking in our dorm, and one of my white roommates asked me, . . . 'Why do all of you guys have all these separate Korean Christian clubs?' He was kind of like asking why can't you Christians all just get along? You would think if anyone could get along it would be [the Christians]." Christian students who take part in the few multiracial Christian fellowships on campus also point a critical finger at separate ethnic ministries, as one of them comments:

> I can understand why they want to have a Vietnamese culture club or KSA [Korean Student's Association], . . . but I don't know why they have to attach Christianity to ethnicity. Would Jesus do it? If he came back today, where would Jesus go? If he came back as a twenty-year-old white guy at WU, would he be accepted in these Korean Christian fellowships?

The onus to be ethnically inclusive is present because SGKAs are Christians, but it is also present because SGKAs do not "have to be" ethnically segregated to practice their faith.

One of the complaints that SGKAs have against the first generation's ethnic church is their ethnic exclusivity—the fact that the church is closed off from the rest of the ethnically diverse community. SGKAs in separate ethnic campus ministries, however, find themselves in the same predicament. In contrast to the mainly first-generation alumni of the fellowships, who are the most adamant about maintaining a monoethnic identity for the fellowships, many SGKAs grew up in diverse neighborhoods with ethnically and racially diverse friends. Their services are conducted in English, they meet at a convenient location on campus, and they adhere to a universal religion that strongly emphasizes proselytizing nonbelievers, whatever the race.

Recognizing this, some Korean American leaders of campus ministries note that they have no real justification for having separate ethnic ministries. An SGKA student leader of KAMC laments: "We have no excuse like our parents. I don't see the point of like KAMC and CSF for second gen[eration]s. I mean, I like my [Korean American campus fellowship], but just because you are in it does not mean you think it is OK. You are not doing what Jesus said you should be doing." Another Korean American comments that ethnic boundary distinctions are not necessary for the later generations: "The barriers are not as big as people think they are. Why do people form KAMC? Because they are so used to going to Korean churches for all of their lives, so naturally they form it without thinking about it. But they don't really need to do it. I don't see any real boundary. . . . We just need to get over what we are used to."

This tension can intensify when Korean American students attempt to evangelize different ethnic groups. Two SGKA students from KAMC share how they were conflicted when they evangelized a white woman who not only wanted to hear "the gospel message" but also wanted to join their campus ministry. If a Korean American woman had expressed interest in joining their campus ministry, the two students would have readily and eagerly invited her to KAMC. But because the student was white, they were hesitant and troubled. One of the two students ex- plains, "I felt awkward . . . embarrassed, because I didn't want to invite her out to KAMC because I knew that she would feel like an outcast or feel different because everyone basically looks the same [at KAMC]." The other SGKA student who had also evangelized the white woman says he went ahead and invited her to KAMC but forewarned her that most of the members are Korean American. Because of this, the student suspects that the white woman did not contact him again. He explains: "It is kind of hard to invite people to KAMC . . . even that one [white] girl, she said, 'I will come out,' but inside I felt kind of uncomfortable, so I told her that I would love for you to come out, but we are all Ko- rean people. She said she would e-mail us, but she never did. . . . I really regret that I could not help her more." Had these two students been part of a more ethnically diverse campus ministry, they would not have hesitated to invite her to their campus ministry, and it is more likely that the student would have accepted their invitation and joined them. Thus, the ethnically separate nature of SGKA Evangelicals' religious participa- tion conflicts with their more inclusive faith.

The leaders are usually the ones who talk about the tension. Further- more, it is the professionally trained clergy leaders who are the most ad- amant about moving toward a multiethnic ministry. The clerical leader for CSF trained at Evangelical institutions (Biola University and Fuller Theological Seminary), which place an emphasis on cross-cultural evan- gelism. His advocacy of a multiethnic approach generated a lot of strife with the other staff members. The biggest conflict came when he sought to drop the ethnically distinguishable moniker of the campus ministry —changing the name from "Korean" Christian Fellowship to simply Christian Student Fellowship.

This tension, however, is not equally experienced by SGKAs in separate ethnic ministries. Some occasionally talk about it but emphasize that it is not something they dwell on. Others claim to never have experienced such tensions (though they recognize that it does or could exist). As a Korean American student puts it, "Most people do not think about it . . . for most people having intellectual or theological coherence is not an issue." Another Korean American student leader points out:

> Do you think the average freshmen coming here, maybe just looking for a few friends, good time, hang out . . . nervous about if he is going to fit in or not is going to think about that? . . . Nah, man. At the maturity level of people coming here, as freshmen, their first opinion is not going to be like "OK, I am going to worship God with the whole family of Christ." Instead it is like [CSF] is cool, I am going to try it out.

Some campus Evangelicals further note that the majority of people do not have the time to think about such conflicts when faced with the practical realities of being part of a campus ministry as busy college students. A student leader of KAMC shares: "We can barely keep up with the people that are in our own campus ministry. Trying to help them as students ourselves is hard enough, so we don't have time to even begin to think about things like [the tension], even though I admit it is a problem."

The tension between separation and integration is thus not equally experienced by SGKA Evangelicals, and some may not experience it at all. But it is a tension that SGKAs, particularly those in leadership, recognize and sense. In today's increasingly diverse society, it is a conflict that all of the ethnic Christian congregations that attract a native-born population, whether on or off campus, will face.

Why Christians Can't All Just Get Along

Much of why ethnic and racial segregation persists in the Christian community—why Christians can't all just "get along"—is because ethnicity and religion get along so well. Ethnic separatism and religious universalism may conflict, but ethnicity and religion serve similar functions and reinforce one another in various ways.

Meaning, Identity, Belonging

Religion is particularly good at providing individuals a sense of meaning, identity, and belonging. Classic works from Emile Durkheim's *Elementary Forms of Religion*[2] to more contemporary studies on religious communities continuously show this to be the case (Bellah 1970; Durkheim 1995; Greeley 1972; Herberg 1955; Kwon et al. 1997; Min 1992; Smith 1978; Vecoli 1977; Zhou et al. 2002). Peter Berger (1967) argues that faced with the innate precariousness of the social world, every society is engaged in building a significant world. Religion plays a pivotal role in creating a cultural web of meaning in our society; it "has a strategic part in the human enterprise of world-building" (Berger 1967: 27).

As previously discussed, immigrant churches play an important part in providing Korean immigrants a sense of meaning, place, and identity. The ethnic church is where Korean immigrants find a sense of belonging, value, and shelter. It is their über community. Studies on other ethnic groups find the same.

In his study of Southern Italian immigrants at the turn of the twentieth century, Rudolph Vecoli found that religion is one of the important "tried and true ways of coping with the great Unknown" and of helping immigrants to deal with the various challenges that they confront in the new country (1977: 33). Similarly, Will Herberg's study of Protestant, Catholic, and Jewish immigrants concludes that religion operates as the "meaningful center of life"; it provides immigrants with a "fundamental way of 'adjusting' and 'belonging'" (1955: 72). Religion helps them figure out who they are.

We have also seen the important role that campus ministries take in providing minority and majority students alike a significant sense of identity and community. Indeed, religion can be the "very cement of social fabric" (Malinowski 1954: 82). Religion, however, is not the only source of meaning and place.

Ethnicity also provides a significant foundation for identity, meaning, and community. According to the primordial theory of ethnicity, racial and ethnic distinctions have been salient and have commonly demarcated the lines of intergroup conflict throughout history because racial and ethnic distinctions are the basic group identity of mankind. They are deeply engrained in the very nature of human sociality (van den

Berghe 1981, 1990). Ethnic ties are extensions of kinship affinities, and ethnic alliances form because they advance the interests of those who are thought to have common descent.

While the notion that ethnicity is primordial in nature is disputable, there is consensus that ethnicity provides people with meaning, identity, and community (Abramson 1973; Bankston and Zhou 1995; Gans 1979; Greeley 1974; Yancey et al. 1976). In fact, ethnicity, by its very definition, is based on the idea of a group with a shared cultural identity, language, and origin. The word "ethnic" is an adjective that is derived from the Greek noun *ethnos,* which means people or nations. An ethnic group is commonly connected by a shared heritage and a sense of peoplehood. Ethnicity itself is community and identity.

Putting the similar functions of religion and ethnicity together, we can thus conclude that groups that are both ethnic and religious have a stronger basis for meaning construction, cohesion, and group identity. As we have seen, ethnic religious organizations enable individuals to find meaningful community and forge not only a religious but also an emergent ethnic identity. It helps SGKAs construct an identity and community that is all their own. Thus, separation persists in part because ethnicity and religion perform similar desirable functions and provide a stronger basis for meaningful group identity.

Rational Choice

According to the basic theory of rational choice, individuals seek to maximize benefits and minimize costs. Presuming this goal is what individuals seek, a religious organization that offers both religious and ethnic goods can attract more religious consumers. An ethnic religious organization can specialize and more strategically and productively attract consumers, as individuals can be drawn to the group for not only religious but also ethnic reasons.[3]

This approach is evident in campus pastors' and leaders' argument that "more souls would be saved" by offering both ethnic and religious goods in campus ministries. As a leader of a campus ministry reflects, "If we did not have contextualized [ethnic] ministries, I guarantee you that some students will not come." If the ethnic component were taken out of campus ministries, it is expected that far fewer members would join and be saved in the process.

Campus pastors explain that this is because most people are not "spiritually mature enough" to worship with the "greater body of Christ":

> Most people coming into campus ministry are not spiritually mature. So when you are trying to reach them, you want to make sure that you do not place any unnecessary obstacles, barriers, in their way. For example, if you have an African American student who is interested in learning more about Christ, you don't want to bring him into a Korean American campus ministry setting where he is obviously going to be uncomfortable . . . but if he was placed in a contextualized campus ministry for African Americans, you can see how he would have an easier time and grow.

Another also explains: "People are lazy, they want what is easy. . . . They don't want to have to work so hard, especially when they are not at that level of spiritual maturity, so having a Korean American campus ministry where the students would be more comfortable can help."

Because most students are not "spiritually mature" enough to take part in integrated multiracial congregations, pursuing separate ethnic ministries becomes the most reasonable path for campus ministry leaders. To go against the average religious consumers' desire for what is *most* comfortable—ethnic ministries—would risk losing religious customers. Within a competitive religious marketplace, more "souls" would be saved through contextualized ethnic ministries—by combining ethnicity and religion. Thus, separate ethnic ministries become the most rational option.

Shelter

One explanation for religious vitality is the sheltered enclave theory, which argues that religions—particularly traditional, conservative religions—persist and flourish when they are "sheltered" from the obtrusive secularizing forces in modern society (Hunter 1983, 1987). Applying this theory to understand how American Evangelicalism survives and even prospers in contemporary America, James Davidson Hunter (1983, 1987) argues that it thrives because Evangelicals are in their social and demographic location considerably shielded from the religiously obtrusive forces of modernity. Comparing Evangelicals with other populations in America using the 1978–1979 survey data collected by the Princeton Religious Research Center, Hunter (1983) finds that Evangelicals tend to be older, more female, less educated, more married, from lower-income backgrounds, and concentrated more in smaller and rural towns than in urban areas. With these results, Hunter concludes that Evangelicals can thrive in a secularized modern society because they are demographically and socially sheltered in an enclave away from the corrosive effects of modernity.

One of the criticisms against sheltered enclave theory is that most contemporary Evangelicals do not demographically and socially reside in "sheltered enclaves" where their values, beliefs, and practices can be properly protected from outside secular forces. Many, like the growing numbers of Asian American college Evangelicals, are in fact immersed in one of the most secular institutions in the United States. With this criticism in mind, however, it cannot be denied that religious organizations attempt to and can be successful in providing a form of "shelter" from the secularizing forces in the broader society. By regularly bringing together people of like minds and religious worldviews, religious organizations help people maintain their faith. Even if Evangelicals are not demographically segregated from the rest of the population, they can be socially and emotionally sheltered from some of the secular challenges to their faith.

That is what Paul A. Bramadat (2000) found in his in-depth ethnography of an IVCF chapter at McMaster University in Ontario. He found that IVCF functions as an alternative institution, enabling students to work through the social spiritual estrangement and sense of "otherness" that they experience as they relate themselves to their secular peers. IVCF offers a unique Evangelical counterpart to every secular student social function and organizes meetings and events that help students address the cognitive and social dissonance that they face as Evangelical Christians in a secular setting. Bramadat found that, far from being ghettoized, IVCF members are actively engaged in campus life and IVCF functions as a bridge to facilitate a friendly and constructive rapport between its students and non-Christians. Thus, IVCF provides shelter and helps its members maintain their faith and thrive as Evangelicals in an otherwise secular environment. This is evident on the WU campus as well.

Campus ministries at WU have various activities that keep students occupied and steer them away from the more profane activities that occupy their secular peers. It is no coincidence that Korea-Campus Crusade for Christ has all-night prayer gatherings on Friday nights—the time when students are most likely to pursue this-worldly pleasures. And Asian American Christian Fellowship has events like the "secular music fast," where students are encouraged to listen to Christian music and abstain from listening to secular music. All of the campus ministries also have "retreats" where students can "retreat" into the woods or to a nearby beach to socialize and revive their faith. Additionally, there are lunch and dinner gatherings, sports events, prayer meetings, Bible studies, field trips, and more that can occupy students' spare time.

The importance of "accountability" within campus ministries further demonstrates that campus ministries help foster and maintain students' faith in an otherwise secular setting. Women who are in serious dating relationships talk about how accountability and strong social ties with like-minded co-religious friends prevent them from engaging in premarital sex. Meanwhile, men in small Bible study groups talk about how they can overcome the temptation to view internet pornography by "keeping each other accountable." Students involved in campus ministries commonly room together, and older student leaders function as senior accountability partners to help the younger members successfully maneuver themselves in a secular college environment.

Campus ministries also help students grapple with and even overcome some of the secular challenges to their faith. Veritas Forum is a good example of this. Originally started in 1992 by several graduate students at Harvard University, Veritas Forums have now been held on over fifty campuses throughout the United States. One of the campuses that regularly holds these forums is WU.

Guided by the national Veritas Forum team and created by local university ministers, professors, and students, Veritas Forums are university-wide events that seek to enlarge the university's marketplace of ideas and present Jesus Christ as a viable option to life's hardest questions. Some of the topics that are explored at the forums have included "The Journey: A Thinking Person's Quest for Meaning," "What Does It Mean to Be Human?," "Big Bang, Stephen Hawking, and God," "Time for Truth: Living Free in a World of Lies, Hype, and Spin," "The Power of Porn, the Power of Love," "Islam and Christianity," "Scientific Evidence for the Existence of God," "Educating for Liberty: The Principles and Pitfalls of Teaching Character and Virtue in an Age of Diversity," "10 Questions Intellectuals Ask about Christianity," "Problems of Evil:

Does the Fact of Evil in Some Way Disprove God's Existence?," "The Call: Finding and Fulfilling the Central Purpose of Your Life," "The Cultural Phenomenon of Falling in Love," "The Historical Jesus: A Dialogue of a Theist and an Agnostic Humanist," and "Where Genesis and Science Intersect."[4] The forums encourage Evangelical Christian students to maintain and even invigorate their faith in a setting where liberalism, scientific reasoning, and diverse worldviews reign.

In addition to the support and shelter that campus ministries provide from secularism, campus ministries shield their members from marginalization as ethnic and racial minorities. As discussed, ethnic campus ministries not only offer an alternative Christian social enclave but also provide empowerment and refuge from prejudice, racism, and any general discomfort that an individual may experience as an ethnic or racial minority. Thus, another reason separation persists despite the call for universalism is because ethnic and religious ties perform similar functions. They empower individuals and shelter them from the marginalization that they may confront in the broader society as Christians, as well as ethnic and racial minorities.

Negotiating the Conflict in Everyday Life

Aside from the intimate connection between ethnicity and religion, separation persists because individuals make practical attempts to mitigate the tension between ethnic separatism and religious universalism in daily life. Within the Evangelical campus community, I found that this is done in three ways that underscore the significance of choice and comfort in primary group ties.

Choice

As discussed, SGKAs are concerned that the ethnically homogenous nature of their campus ministries may repel non–Korean Americans, who may otherwise be interested in the Christian religion, from participating in campus ministry. Conflicts arise when SGKAs in separate ethnic campus ministries "outreach" and evangelize non–Korean Americans who want not only to convert but also to take part in a campus ministry. Problems occur when SGKAs share the gospel with "all nations" but then cannot invite "all nations" into their campus ministries.

This tension, however, is practically assuaged by the knowledge that there are other campus ministries that non–Korean Americans can attend. As an SGKA states, "So long as we are not the only campus ministry out there . . . I think it is OK." Other SGKA students similarly comment: "I mean it is best that they go to the campus group where they feel the most comfortable and where they think they can grow . . . so if this is not for them, then they can go somewhere else. . . . It is not like KAMC is the only campus ministry around." Another SGKA explains: "There are so many other groups on campus, so if they did want to learn the gospel here . . . there are so many other resources, other places that they can turn to. So I don't feel that bad about it." SGKAs thus negotiate the tension between their separatism and religious universalism by acknowledging the choices that individuals have in their religious participation—that they are not the only campus ministries that people can attend.

"We Are All Sinners . . ."

Some Korean Americans explain the seeming contradiction between their religious beliefs and their ethnic exclusivity by noting that people are naturally weak and "sinful" and fail to do what is right. "How do we deal with it? I don't know . . . it is just sin, we are weak," one student says. "We know what is good, what is right, but we don't do it." Another SGKA student explains that the weakness extends to Christians in general:

> I know it is sad, but that is just the way it has always been. . . . Like I know these Christian guys at [a Christian university], you would think that they would be different. I mean one of them wants to be a pastor, but they watch all this porn. . . . It was so bad [my friend's boyfriend] who lived with them had to just move out, it was such a bad environment. . . . Christians are definitely not perfect, or there are a lot of phony ones out there.

Given the "sinful" and "fallen" nature of man, Evangelicals are not surprised that people have little trouble dealing with the apparent contradictions between their religious beliefs and religious practice. As a white student leader of a campus ministry explains: "How would they deal with it? They don't. How many homeless people do we walk by and not even flinch? It is such hypocrisy. You would think that if there is one thing that is pure, it is religion, but because it involves people, fallen man, it is not easy." Thus, the tension between ethnic separatism and religious universalism is negotiated by noting that segregation within the Christian community is only one of men's and women's many weaknesses, inconsistencies, and hypocrisies. In the face of this fact of life, some note that they could only "pray" and "turn to Jesus for help." An SGKA student who started attending a multiethnic church reflects: "We have to pray that Jesus will move their hearts and inspire them to change . . . that the Holy Spirit would work in them. . . . Otherwise, unless Jesus changes people's hearts, change is not going to happen."

The conflict between ethnic separatism and religious universalism is therefore partly alleviated by labeling the problem as a "spiritual" problem that is so inherent that it ultimately will require divine intervention to resolve.[5] In many ways, however, much of what the interview subjects refer to as a "sin problem" really points to individual basic desires for what is most beneficial and comfortable and least costly and painful. What is "sinful" is SGKAs' and others' desire for homophily, majority group status, and escape from marginalization in a social context where ethnic groups are categorized and race continues to matter.

Partial Integration

The leaders and members of ethnic campus ministries also negotiate the tension between separation and integration by having some services that are more inclusive. By having a few of the more public aspects of SGKAs' religious participation more integrated, SGKAs do not feel guilty about having their more private religious fellowship segregated. This is most evident in many of the Evangelical Christian campus ministries' involvement in the Intercollegiate Christian Council (ICC).

Led by student representatives of the various Christian groups on campus, ICC holds several events throughout the school year to unite Christian students at WU and positively impact the overall campus. For example, ICC helped organize the Veritas Forums. They also coordinated events like "Love WU day" where the various Christian groups at WU provided free food and drinks to students on campus in an effort to express "Jesus' love." These sorts of activities enable the members of the different ethnic campus ministries to unite and work together and experience what it is like to be part of a larger Christian community, as SGKA students explain:

> The first time [an ICC event] was held, . . . you walked in and there was this room full of Christians from all the fellowships . . . and most of them were represented. The major ones were all there, and we were worshipping and praying together as an entire body. There was so much power in that . . . thousands of voices praising God. It was an awesome experience.

> ICC is where you can get out of your bubble, do something crazy for this campus . . . like on Love WU day, we passed out food and drinks to whoever as a group.

> I was really excited with [one of the events supported by the ICC]. . . . It was so good to see groups getting together to repent and worship together. I really loved meeting non–Korean Christians.

> It is cool to have your own personal fellowship where you can get along better, but I really like something like ICC, where you can see God work as a whole body of Christians at school instead of just at CSF. It definitely helps you to think bigger . . . it gets you out of your little niche.

Participating in ICC and its events thus enables students to unite and take part in the broader Christian community while maintaining their more intimate primary ethnic group ties. SGKAs can alleviate the guilt that they may have over their private separatism by noting that they occasionally unite with the "whole body of Christ"—that they are not entirely exclusive in their religious participation.

The tension between ethnic separatism and religious universalism is further negotiated by having some activities that are more inclusive *within* each of the ethnic campus ministries. While both KAMC and CSF are separate ethnic campus ministries for SGKAs, they also have religious activities within their organization that include other ethnic and racial groups. They feed the homeless, work at local charities, and go on short-term mission trips to foreign countries like Mexico, Kazakhstan, and China. By participating in these activities, students within separate ethnic campus ministries have opportunities to extend beyond their ethnic communities and mitigate the tension that comes from their separatism. A student leader of KAMC describes how KAMC is trying to step beyond the "Korean Christian bubble":

> We are trying to help people to have a bigger vision . . . look beyond the Korean Christian bubble. . . . So like now, the core [the KAMC leadership] is trying to get together with this environmental group on campus and do like a homeless thing. We also want to do stuff for the community in general and also the WU community for us to say, at least we are trying. At least people can see that, as a Christian group, we are trying to break down barriers and not have these walls so strong and so big. It is tough, but I think that it is something that we have to press.

SGKAs can thus assuage the unease that they may feel about their separatism by making some of their more public religious services inclusive. SGKAs can be satisfied that not all of their religious participation is segregated.

Conclusion

Why can't Evangelical Christians overcome ethnic and racial divisions and "just get along?" Part of the reason is because ethnicity and religion work so well together. Ethnicity and religion perform similar functions and positively reinforce each other. Within a competitive religious marketplace, an ethnic campus ministry can specialize and more easily mobilize and attract members. It can draw consumers seeking either ethnic or religious goods, or both. Ethnic religious organizations can provide a stronger basis for meaningful community and group identity. And they can shelter their members from marginalization that comes from being a Christian as well as an ethnic minority.

Besides the intimate connections between ethnicity and religion, individuals make various practical attempts to negotiate the conflict between ethnic separatism and religious universalism. If SGKAs are uneasy about inviting non–Korean Americans to their campus ministries, they can be assured that non–Korean Americans can go to the variety of other campus ministries available in the religious marketplace. The fact that potential religious consumers can turn to a number of other campus ministries ranging in ethnic diversity makes it "OK" that they are ethnically exclusive.

SGKAs also talk of the "sinful nature of man," man's desire for what is *most* comfortable, to justify or explain their separation to themselves and others. The tension between ethnic separatism and religious universalism is negotiated by noting that segregation within the Christian community is only one of men's and women's many weaknesses, inconsistencies, and hypocrisies that ultimately will require divine intervention to resolve. Additionally, SGKAs soothe the guilt that they may have over their exclusivity by making some of their more public religious services inclusive. These attempts, which reveal the importance of choice and personal comfort at the primary group level, make it possible for Christians to maintain separate ethnic group boundaries despite Christ's resounding call for unity.

Conclusion

A New Theory of Emergent Ethnicity

The incorporation of today's "successful" children of immigrants into U.S. society is captured by neither assimilation nor ethnic retention. Socioeconomic mobility, along with entrance into the clubs and institutions of host society at the primary group level, is not leading to the expected weakening of ethnic ties. Instead of dissolving, it is precisely on the path of assimilation and primary group contact that ethnic "groupness" becomes strengthened. The ethnicity that emerges from this interaction, however, is not the "old" ethnicity inherited from the first generation. Instead, it is an emergent ethnicity "made in the U.S.A."

We have seen that little is actually retained from the first generation by the second generation in terms of their religious participation. Ethnic values and cultures of the first generation are not what constitute SGKAs' religious services. SGKAs draw the sharpest boundaries between themselves and the first generation, and their campus ministries are modeled after mainstream campus ministries and look more like them than either the first-generation ethnic church or campus ministries. Furthermore, characteristics that can be deemed uniquely "Korean American" about SGKAs' religious services are often picked up and adopted by the mainstream campus ministries. In a diverse and competitive religious marketplace, Korean Americans and other Asian Americans are innovating ways of doing campus ministries. All of this, however, does not then mean that SGKAs are "assimilating."

SGKAs' campus ministries are similar to mainstream campus ministries, and they share much with other native-born ethnic groups. However, given the choice, they will turn to ethnic-specific over pan-ethnic, multiracial, or predominately white campus ministries. SGKAs will congregate with those who are *most* like themselves—those who are most likely to share similar and familiar experiences of growing up with intergenerational and intercultural conflicts with the first generation Koreans in America. Thus, what draws SGKAs together at the primary group level and qualifies as the "Korean American" experience is constructed in America.

The finding that ethnicity is emergent and "made in the U.S.A." is not new. There is consensus that the "so-called foreign heritage" of immigrants is constructed and reinvented in America (Conzen et al. 1992; Handlin 1951; Sollors 1991). But just how and why ethnicity is reinvented and remains salient for later generations remains open to debate.

Having first coined the term "emergent ethnicity," Yancey et al. (1976) reject assimilationist arguments regarding the temporarily persistent nature of ethnicity as well as pluralist arguments regarding cultural heritages as the basis of ethnic group solidarity. Instead, they argue that ethnicity becomes solidified under the structural conditions of "residential stability and segregation, common occupational positions and dependence on local institutions and services" (Yancey et al. 1976: 399). Emergent ethnicities take shape within the structural parameters that characterize urban working-class life with the residential, occupational, and institutional concentration of ethnic groups.

Yancey et al.'s (1976) structural argument regarding the construction of emergent ethnicities is posed as an alternative to assimilation and pluralist theories. Their argument, however, is similar to assimilation theories that view ethnicity as a working-class phenomenon. Assimilation theorists, including segmented assimilation theorists, would agree that ethnic identities and associations will be strong among immigrants who are under the structural conditions that characterize urban working-class life. But they would argue that ethnicity would lose significance once immigrants, particularly the later generations, move outside of the urban ethnic ghetto and gain entrance into the institutions and organizations of the "host society." While Yancey et al. would not agree with the latter point regarding the decline and disappearance of ethnicity, they likewise do not seriously consider how emergent ethnicities would be constructed beyond the ethnic ghetto, particularly for the later generations. Yancey et al. do not explain just how ethnicity changes for the children of immigrants and what may or may not be retained from past generations.

Focusing on the structural conditions that promote ethnic group formation, Yancey et al. (1976) fail to address what draws individuals to form ethnic group identities and associations in the first place. Having rejected explanations regarding the salience of cultural heritages, they do not offer any alternative explanation for why individuals would identify and associate ethnically when given the structural opportunity to do so.

In contrast to Yancey et al. (1976) and assimilation theorists, my research shows that ethnic "groupness" can be strengthened and reactively formed beyond the ethnic ghetto. I find that emergent ethnicities can be constructed precisely as the children of today's immigrants come into primary contact with the majority group in the mainstream institutions and organizations of the host society. Unlike the overly structural argument presented by Yancey and his colleagues, I argue that this emergent ethnicity is the product of both micro-level and macrostructural factors. Moreover, I argue that emergent ethnic group formation is not unique to SGKAs and other ethnic minorities. Whites create their own emergent ethnic identity for essentially the same reasons that ethnic minorities do.

Interactive Micro- and Macroconditions of Emergent Ethnicity Construction

Micro-Level Conditions

The findings of this study illuminate three micro-level individual factors that are involved in the construction of emergent ethnicities. First, individuals want to belong—to have friends, significant other(s), and community. On or off the college campus, people want to be more than their social security and driver's license numbers; they want to be known and connected to a meaningful community.

Second, at the primary group level, individuals want to associate with those who are most familiar and similar to them and follow the homogenous principle. Given the choice, they will associate with those with whom they have the *most* similar cultural and familial experiences.

Third, individuals want to be the majority group in power and have the respect and status that comes with it. As college students who have gained access to top universities and entered into formerly white-dominant campus ministries, SGKAs feel entitled. They want the benefits and resources that are accorded to their perceived level of achievement; they want to have the power and status that the white majority enjoys and avoid any marginalization that may come from being an ethnic minority.

These micro-level factors interact with three macro-structural conditions to construct emergent ethnicities.

Macro-Level Conditions

First, individual desire for community interacts with social structural opportunities—changes in the ethnic density and diversity of U.S. society—to make separate ethnic associations, including ethnic religious organizations, simply more possible. In an ethnically dense and multicultural setting where explorations and expressions of ethnicity are encouraged, individuals seeking friends, significant other(s), and "fellowship" have greater opportunities to congregate with other co-ethnics.

Second, individual desires for what is most familiar and similar interact with ethnic and racial categorizations. The U.S. government, educational institutions, businesses, media, and individuals in everyday life continue to use ethnic and racial categorizations. A Korean American living in U.S. society cannot escape being categorized as "Korean" or "Asian," no matter how he or she may want to be categorized. This reality pushes individuals to identify ethnically and racially, and it strengthens ethnic ties and the basis for ethnic homophily.

Third, individual desires for power and majority status interact with the continuing marginalization of people categorized as belonging to a particular ethnic or racial group. Conflict, rather than cooperation and mutual adaptation, ensues as some of the children of today's immigrants obtain socioeconomic mobility and enter into the cliques, organizations, and institutions of the host society. Contrary to what assimilationists like Robert E. Park would argue, "human cooperation and interpersonal intimacy" do not replace competition and the tendency for domination to move the "cycle of race relations" naturally toward assimilation (1950: 150).

The group that is newest to the scene wants to be accepted by the members of the host society without having to make the kind of one-sided changes that characterizes traditional views of unilateral assimilation. They do not want to have assimilation simply "done to them" and be the only ones who adapt and adjust in the process of incorporation. And because they have gained entrance into the cliques and organizations of the host society, they want to have the power and status of the majority. Ethnic minorities find that the majority group is unyielding, however.

Whites do not want to share their power and privilege and engage in the kind of mutually affected and adaptive incorporation that would make the minority newcomers comfortable enough to really assimilate at the primary group level. Consequently, the newcomers' chances of gaining mobility and power within the predominately white or even multiracial organizations are limited. SGKAs thus turn to their own co-ethnic congregations. Being in an ethnically homogenous campus ministry of their own means that they can take their ethnicity for granted, enjoy being the majority group in power, and have greater opportunities to take on leadership positions within the congregation. SGKAs do not have to confront prejudice, racism, or any other miscellaneous discomfort that they may experience in the broader society as an ethnic or racial minority.

White Flight and the Construction of Reactive Emergent Ethnicity

When more ethnic minorities start filling the seats in their campus ministry, white students take flight. They leave and construct their own reactive emergent sense of groupness. This happens because whites also want what the ethnic minorities want.

Whites want to keep their campus ministry as it was, predominately white; they want their own homophily and to remain the unquestioned majority. As ethnic minorities challenge and threaten this, whites take flight; they leave in search of campus ministries or comparable organizations where they can maintain their majority status without contest. Thus, the same three interactive processes that make ethnic minorities separate also prompt whites to form and congregate in their own unofficially white associations. The only difference is that whites already have the majority group status and want to maintain it, while ethnic minority groups do not yet have it and want to obtain it.

Interestingly, one of the ways whites maintain their majority group status and create their own unofficially white campus ministries is by simply pointing to ethnic minorities' desires to separate. In the broader university context where multiculturalism and different ethnic heritages are celebrated, leaders of campus ministries do not use overtly racist tactics to maintain power. Instead, they use the rhetoric that ethnic minorities want to segregate and have their own organizations and therefore help them create separate ethnic ministries. In so doing, whites, by default, get to have their own campus ministry—they can have their campus ministry back to what it was before the flood of ethnic minorities entered their campus ministry. Thus, whites are not simply "pushed out" of their organization, and separate ethnic ministries are not created solely for the sake of ethnic minorities. Whites are actively engaged in the separation of campus ministries and the construction of their own, and others', emergent group identities.

Thus, assimilation into the traditional white middle-class is not as easy as assimilation scholars pose it to be once socioeconomic mobility is obtained. Additionally, it is precisely at the point of primary group contact that ethnic group differences become amplified—that conflict, rather than mutual cooperation and understanding, occurs. A sense of ethnic groupness or separateness is activated, and what difference(s) may or may not have existed become accentuated on both sides of the divide. Ethnic minorities create emergent ethnicities, but so does the majority group. Whites create their own reactive emergent ethnicity as they interact with other ethnic groups who are increasingly challenging their majority group power and status.

Crossing Boundaries

In one way or another, all of the SGKAs mention comfort when they explain why they are in separate ethnic ministries over pan-ethnic, multiracial, or predominately white campus ministries. We have seen that this comfort stems from SGKAs simply having more points of convergence with other second-generation co-ethnics relative to other groups. SGKAs have cultural and familial experiences similar to those of other children of immigrants, like second-generation Chinese Americans. But they share more with other SGKAs. Thus, what is essential is the *extent* of convergence. In a context where racial categorizations and racism persist, SGKAs have the *most* similar private and public lived-experiences with fellow second-generation co-ethnics. They will therefore flock to separate ethnic ministries when given the choice to do so.

There are interracial marriages, dating, and friendships that cross ethnic and racial boundaries. There are multiethnic and multiracial campus ministries in addition to ethnically or racially homogenous campus ministries. There are even SGKAs who claim they share more homophily with other ethnic groups and vice versa. Crossing boundaries at the primary group level is possible. But it is more difficult. It is relatively more "uncomfortable."

Going against the tendency to pursue what is most similar and familiar, stepping beyond ethnic and racial categorizations, and compromising one's desire for majority status and escape from marginalization is not easy. We saw that those who cross ethnic boundaries at the intimate group level risk being labeled and treated as deviants from both sides of the ethnic divide. It can be socially and emotionally taxing. Thus, boundaries can be crossed, but given the choice, most people will separate rather than integrate.

Ethnicity and Religion

The topic of assimilation and ethnic group formation does not just concern immigration scholars. More than ever, America's religious communities are debating and pondering whether they should pursue separate ethnic or more integrated multiethnic congregations. Traditionally white mainstream Evangelical organizations wonder whether they should develop separate ethnic ministries for their increasingly diverse membership or pursue multiethnic ministries. Even immigrant ethnic congregations are asking whether they should transition from an ethnically homogenous congregation into a more inclusive and multiethnic one, particularly in light of the increasing numbers of second and third generations.

Evangelicals, on and off the college campus, worry that they are falling short of Jesus' call to preach the gospel to "all nations" and have their church be a "house of prayer for all nations." What is the Christian church communicating to the rest of society when it remains one of the most segregated institutions of America? There is a moral and ethical dilemma between the separatism of their religious practice and the universalism of their faith. This then leads Evangelical Christians to ask, "Why can't we all just get along?"

Part of the answer is because ethnicity and religion actually work well together. They positively reinforce one another and serve similar functions. Both provide meaning, identity, and community. Ethnic religious organizations empower its members and provide refuge from the secular challenges to their faith, and from ethnic and racial marginalization as well. Moreover, in a competitive religious marketplace, ethnic religious organizations have a greater basis for mobilization and can attract members seeking ethnic and/or religious benefits. Thus, pursuing separate ethnic ministries becomes the most reasonable path for religious leaders seeking to attract the most number of congregants.

Separation also remains the norm because individuals make everyday practical attempts to work through the tension between ethnic separatism and religious universalism. Those in ethnically homogenous campus ministries who feel guilty about their separatism can reason that they are not the only campus ministries that interested consumers can take part in; there are plenty of other campus fellowships in the religious marketplace. They can also assuage the unease that they may experience over their separatism by having a few religious activities and services be more ethnically inclusive. And they can always point to the perennial problem of "sin." Multiracial congregations may be ideal, but because humans are fundamentally sinful and flawed creatures, little can be done to pursue integrated congregations.

The intimate connection between ethnicity and religion and these internal rationalizations and negotiations in everyday life then help explain why separate ministries remain the norm—why Sunday mornings are still so segregated.

Where Will They Go after College?

The college years are no doubt an important time for self-exploration, identity formation, and group mobilization. For ethnic minority students, college can be one of the first times that they seriously consider notions of ethnicity and race and its relationship to themselves and others. Accordingly, it could be argued that my findings regarding emergent ethnic group formation is largely a college phenomenon—unlikely to be replicated or continued in the "real world" beyond the college campus. This, however, is not likely, given that the three interactive processes which I argue help to construct emergent ethnicities can be found in the larger society as well.

Desires for community, homophily, and majority power and status do not end on the college campus. On or off the college campus, individuals seek friendships, significant other(s), and community; what is most familiar and similar; and majority status, empowerment, and escape from marginalization. Structural changes in ethnic density and diversity, ethnic and racial categorizations, and marginalization are also found in greater America.

According to the 2000 U.S. Census, Asian and Pacific Islander Americans made up 12 percent of Los Angeles County, nearly 10 percent of New York City, 8 percent in Boston, and over 13 percent in Seattle Washington (Barnes and Bennett 2002: 7). Asian American children now live in neighborhoods with much higher proportions of co-ethnics than was the case a decade ago: "In metro areas where Asians are more than 4% of the suburban population, the average Asian now lives in a neighborhood that is 16% Asian, up from 12% in 1990" (Logan 2001: 10). As of the year 2000, there were 186,350 Korean Americans in Los Angeles County (CA), 62,130 in Queens County (NY), and 55,573 in Orange County (CA) (U.S. Census 2000; Yu and Choe 2000: 16). SGKAs and other Asian Americans thus have greater opportunities for co-ethnic associations in an increasingly multiethnic and ethnically dense America.

Along with structural changes in ethnic density, there is now a greater awareness, acceptance, and promotion of ethnic diversity and multiculturalism in the American public sphere. Up until the 1960s, the dominant social policy in the United States was Anglo conformity. Since the early 1970s, however, all levels of government have changed their policies to cultural pluralism (Hu-Dehart 1994). Such changes can contribute to ethnic group identification and mobilization beyond the college campus, particularly as ethnic and racial marginalization persists in broader society.[1]

Additionally, technological advances in communication and transportation make co-ethnic identification and association simply more possible.[2] More than ever, individuals in today's technologically advanced global internet and information society have the symbolic and practical competence to forge ethnic cultures. They can continuously innovate and develop a renewed sense of ethnic "groupness" as they travel physically and virtually between and among multiple cultures. For these reasons, SGKAs will continue to construct emergent ethnic identities and ties beyond the college campus, which will no doubt shape the kind of religious organizations that they will call their home in the future.[3]

Appendix A

Interview Questions

A. *Interview Questions for SGKA Students in SGKA Campus Ministries*

What is your current class level (freshmen, sophomore, junior, senior, or other)?

Were you born in the U.S.? If not, when did you immigrate?

Where did you grow up? Where were you raised? What was the ethnic/racial make-up of your neighborhood? What was the ethnic/racial make-up of your elementary school, junior high school, and high school?

How did you get involved in ___? How long have you been involved in ___?

What is your role at ___? Do you hold any leadership positions?

What sort of activities and events do you have at ___?

What do the members usually do after the weekly worship services?

How is ___ organized? Does ___ have an evangelizing event? If so, who do you witness to and how?

Were you active in church before college? What kind of church was it (e.g., a Korean church)? Do you attend church now? What kind of church is it? Do your parents attend a Korean church?

Were most of your friends before college Christians? What were the ethnicities of most of your pre-college friends (e.g. mostly white, Asian, Korean, mixed)? What are the ethnicities of most of your friends now? Would you marry a non-Korean, Asian, non-Asian?

Why did you choose to attend ___ over other campus ministries (e.g., AACF, IVCF, CCC)? Why did you choose to participate in a "Korean" American campus ministry?

How do you think ___ is different from other campus ministries (e.g., AACF, IVCF, CCC of different ethnic/racial make-up)? How do you think ___ is similar to other campus ministries (e.g., AACF, IVCF, CCC of different ethnic/racial make-up)?

What do you think ___ will be like 5–10 years down the road (e.g., remain Korean American)?

What happens when non-Koreans come to ___? Are there any non-Korean Americans at ___? What do you think brings Asian Americans together?

Do you think multiracial campus ministries are rare on campus?

Why do you think there are so many Korean Americans in campus ministries?

How are campus ministries different from churches (e.g., first-generation Korean church)?

What is "Korean" about ___? How is the second generations' worship different from the first generations' in your estimation?

How do you think participating in ___ has affected your college experience?

Do you plan on continuing with some sort of Christian organization after you graduate? What do you think about the "Silent Exodus"? (Explain term if they do not know its meaning.)

What does it mean to be an evangelical Christian?

What does it mean to be a Korean American? What does it mean to be an American?

What separates Korean Americans from whites? What about with other ethnic groups (e.g., blacks, Mexicans, other Asian Americans)?

Do you feel any conflict over being a Christian and being in a separate Korean American campus ministry? If so, what do you do (if anything) to deal with that conflict?

Do you feel any conflict as a Christian attending a secular university?

What is the dating scene like at ___? Do many people date within and outside of ___? What are the norms regarding dating and romantic relationships between men and women? Are issues regarding dating, sex, and marriage discussed within the campus ministry? Do you think there are any gender differences at ___ in terms of worship, organization, and leadership?

*Ask other questions based on leads.

B. *Interview Questions for Non–Korean American Students in Non–Korean American Campus Ministries*

What is your current class level (freshmen, sophomore, junior, senior, or other)?

Were you born in the U.S.?

Where did you grow up? Where were you raised?

How did you get involved in ___? How long have you been involved in ___?

What is your role at ___? (For example, do you hold any leadership positions?)

What sort of activities and events do you have at ___ (e.g., Bible study groups, prayer meetings, sports events)? What do the members usually do after the weekly worship services? How is ___ organized?

Does ___ have an evangelizing event? If so, who do you witness to and how?

Were you active in church before college? What about your parents?

Were most of your pre-college friends Christians?

What were the ethnicities of most of your friends before college? What are the ethnicities of most of your friends now? Would you marry someone of a different ethnicity or race?

Why did you choose to attend ___ over the variety of other campus ministries on campus?

How do you think ___ is different from other campus ministries? How do you think ___ is similar to other campus ministries?

For those who participate in multiracial campus ministries only:

What makes ___ a multiethnic or multiracial campus ministry? What is "multiethnic" or "multiracial" about ___?

For those who participate in pan-ethnic Asian American campus ministries only:

What happens when non–Asian Americans come to ___? Are there any non–Asian Americans at ___? What is "Asian American" about ___?

For those who participate in predominately white campus ministries only:

Why do you think there aren't more non-white students at ___? Why do you think ___ has so many white students?

Why do you think multiracial campus ministries are so rare on campus?

Why do you think there are so many Asian Americans in campus ministries?

How are campus ministries different from churches?

How do you think participating in ____ has affected your college experience?

Do you plan on continuing with some sort of Christian organization after you graduate?

What does it mean to be an evangelical Christian?

What does it mean to be an American?

Do you feel any conflict as a Christian attending a secular university?

What is the dating scene like at ___? Do many people date within and outside of ___? What are the norms regarding dating and romantic relationships between men and women? Are issues regarding dating, sex, and marriage discussed within the campus ministry? Do you think there are any gender differences at ___ in terms of worship, organization, and leadership?

*Ask other questions based on leads.

C. Interview Questions for SGKA Students in Non–Korean American Campus Ministries

What is your current class level (freshmen, sophomore, junior, senior, or other)?

Were you born in the U.S.? If not, when did you immigrate?

Where did you grow up? Where were you raised?

What was the ethnic/racial make-up of your elementary school, junior high school, high school?

How did you get involved in ___? How long have you been involved in ___?

What is your role at ___? Do you hold any leadership positions?

What sort of activities and events do you have at ___?

What do the members usually do after the weekly worship services?

How is ___ organized?

Does ___ have an evangelizing event? If so, who do you witness to and how?

Were you active in church before college? What about your parents?

Were most of your pre-college friends Christians? What were the ethnicities of most of your pre-college friends (e.g., mostly white, Asian, Korean, mixed)? What are the ethnicities of most of your friends now? Would you marry a Korean, Asian, non-Asian?

Why did you choose to attend ___ over other Korean American campus ministries?

How do you think ___ is different from other campus ministries? How do you think ___ is similar to other campus ministries?

What do you think brings Asian Americans together?

Why do you think multiracial campus ministries are so rare on campus?

What do you think ___ will be like 5–10 years down the road?

Why do you think there are so many Korean Americans in campus ministries?

How are campus ministries different from churches (e.g., first-generation Korean church)?

How do you think participating in ___ has affected your college experience?

Do you plan on continuing with some sort of Christian organization after you graduate? What do you think about the "Silent Exodus"? (Explain term if they do not know its meaning.)

What does it mean to be an evangelical Christian?

What does it mean to be a Korean American? What does it mean to be an American?

What separates Korean Americans from whites? What about with other ethnic groups (e.g., blacks, Mexicans)?

What is the dating scene like at ___? Do many people date within and outside of ___? What are the norms regarding dating and romantic relationships between men and women? Are issues regarding dating, sex, and marriage discussed within the campus ministry? Do you think there are any gender differences at ___ in terms of worship, organization, and leadership?

*Ask other questions based on leads.

D. Interview Questions for Korean American Staff/Pastors/Non-student Leaders

Were you born in the U.S.? If not, when did you immigrate?

How did you get involved in ___? What is your position or title at ___?

How long have you served as ___?

What is the general history of the organization? (Ask if they have a written history.)

What are the main goals (mission statement) or focus of ___?

Is there a particular group that ___ targets?

How was the organization founded?

How has the organization changed over the years?

What kind of campus ministry is it—is it evangelical?

How is this campus ministry different from a church and from other campus ministries?

Does it get any financial support from a larger organization (e.g., a church or another larger campus evangelical organization)?

Are most of the students Christians before they join ___?

What is the leadership structure of ___? How is the campus ministry organized?

What is the dating scene like at ___? Do many people date within and outside of ___? What are the norms regarding dating and romantic relationships between men and women? Are issues regarding dating, sex, and marriage discussed within the campus ministry?

Does ___ have an evangelizing event? If so, who do you witness to and how?

Is there any competition with the other campus ministries?

How is ___ different from a first-generation campus ministry?

What happens to students' religious participation after they graduate? What, if anything, do you do to prepare them for life after college in terms of their religious participation?

How do you think participating in ___ shapes students' college experience? What about their lives after college?

What is the ethnic/racial background of most students at ___?

In what ways is ___ a "Korean" American campus ministry?

What happens when students bring non-Koreans to ___? What happens when non-Koreans come to ___?

Do you feel any conflict being ethnic-specific as a Christian campus ministry? If so, what (if anything) do you or the organization do about it?

Why do you think there are so many ethnic-specific campus ministries?

What are the strengths of this ministry? What are the weaknesses?

What vision do you have for ___? How do you see ___ 5–10 years from now?

What do you think it means to be "Korean American"? What does it mean to be American?

What does it mean to be an evangelical Christian?

*Ask other questions based on leads.

E. Interview Questions for Non–Korean American Staff/Pastors/Non-student Leaders

Were you born in the U.S.?

How did you get involved in ___? How long have you served as ___?

What is the general history of the organization? (Ask if they have a written history.)

What are its main goals (mission statement) or focus?

Is there a particular group that ___ targets on campus?

How was the organization founded? How has the organization changed over the years?

What kind of campus ministry is it (e.g., is it evangelical)? In what way is it evangelical?

How is this campus ministry different from a church or from other campus ministries?

Does it get financial or other support from any larger organization (e.g., a church or another larger campus evangelical organization)?

Are most of the students Christians before they join ___?

What is the leadership structure of ___? How is the campus ministry organized?

What is the dating scene like at ___? Do many people date within and outside of ___? What are the norms regarding dating and romantic relationships between men and women? Are issues regarding dating, sex, and marriage discussed within the campus ministry?

Does ___ have an evangelizing event? If so, who do you witness to and how?

Is there any competition with other campus ministries?

What happens to students' religious participation after they graduate? What (if anything) do you do to prepare them for life after college in terms of their religious participation?

How do you think participating in ___ shapes students' college experience? What about their lives after college?

What is the ethnic/racial make-up of ___?

For multiracial campus ministries only:

What makes ___ a multiethnic or multiracial campus ministry? What is "multiethnic" or "multiracial" about ___?

For pan-ethnic Asian American campus ministries only:

What happens when non–Asian Americans come to ___? Are there any non–Asian Americans at ___? What is "Asian American" about ___?

For predominately white campus ministries only:

Why do you think there aren't more non-white students at ___? Why do you think ___ has so many white students?

What are the strengths of your ministry? What are its weaknesses?

What vision do you have for ___?

What does it mean to be American?

What does it mean to be an evangelical Christian?

Appendix B
Letters to Interview/Research Subjects

Letter of Introduction for the Directors/Leaders of the Campus Organizations

Hello, my name is Rebecca. I am a Korean American graduate student in the WU sociology department. I am interested in conducting a study on the growth of Korean American and other Asian American campus evangelical organizations on college campuses. In particular, I am interested in collecting general descriptive information on Korean American and other Asian American campus evangelical organizations, finding out the organizations' major concerns and themes, and exploring some of the reasons behind the growth of Korean American and other Asian American campus evangelical organizations.

Because ___ is one of the largest Korean American (or Asian American) campus evangelical organizations on the WU campus and has chapters on several other college campuses, ___ was selected for study. If I can get your permission to conduct participant observation and interviews in your organization, I would like to participate in your worship services and Bible studies and conduct personal interviews with the college student members and staff of your organization. My study will be conducted for three academic quarters—starting from the Fall 2000 quarter and ending in the Spring 2001 quarter. I would like to interview about ten members from your organization for about 30 minutes to an hour and a half. I will ask questions regarding how they came to participate in your organization and ask them about their involvement in the organization.

By not disclosing the name of your organization and not recording the interview subject's real names, confidentiality will be maintained for your organization and interview subjects. On published records, your organization will be identified as a Korean American or Asian American campus evangelical organization on a large college campus in California and the names of the interview subjects will be changed to maintain confidentiality.

In closing, I would like to ask you for your help and permission to conduct participant observation and interviews in your organization. If you allow me to conduct my study in your organization, I will be more than happy to address any concerns you might have regarding my study and share my findings with you.

Sincerely,
Rebecca Kim

Letter of Introduction for the Directors/Leaders of the Campus Organizations (Non-Asian American)

Hello, my name is Rebecca. I am a graduate student in the WU sociology department. I am interested in conducting a study on the growth of campus evangelical organizations on college campuses. In particular, I am interested in collecting general descriptive information on students' involvement in campus evangelical organizations; finding out campus evangelical organizations' major concerns and themes; and exploring some of the reasons behind its growth in recent years.

Because ___ is one of the largest campus evangelical organizations on the WU campus and has chapters on several other college campuses, ___ was selected for study.

If I can get your permission to conduct participant observation and interviews in your organization, I would like to participate in your worship services and Bible studies and conduct personal interviews with the college student members and staff of your organization. My study will be conducted for three academic quarters—starting from the Fall 2000 quarter and ending in the Spring 2001 quarter. I would like to interview about ten members from your organization for about 30 minutes to an hour and a half. I will ask questions regarding how they came to participate in your organization and ask them about their involvement in the organization.

By not disclosing the name of your organization and not recording the interview subject's real names, confidentiality will be maintained for your organization and interview subjects. On published records, your organization will be identified as a campus evangelical organization on a large college campus in California and the names of the interview subjects will be changed to maintain confidentiality.

In closing, I would like to ask you for your help and permission to conduct participant observation and interviews in your organization. If you allow me to conduct my study in your organization, I will be more than happy to address any concerns you might have regarding my study and share my findings with you.

Sincerely,
Rebecca Kim

Appendix C
Interview/Research Consent Forms

Consent to Participate in Research: Campus Evangelical Organizations

You are asked to participate in a research study conducted by Rebecca Kim, from the sociology department at the University of XX as part of dissertation research. You were selected as a possible participant in this study because you are a staff and/or a member of a campus evangelical organization and have some knowledge and experience with campus evangelical organizations.

PURPOSE OF THE STUDY

The purpose of the study is to gather general descriptive information on campus evangelical organizations and find out the major concerns and themes of such organizations. How and why students came to participate in campus evangelical organizations is also the subject of this study.

PROCEDURES

If you volunteer to participate in this study, I will interview you for approximately 30 minutes to an hour and a half at a location of your choice near campus and ask you questions regarding your involvement in campus ministry.

POTENTIAL RISKS AND DISCOMFORTS

Your participation in this study is voluntary. You may refuse to answer any question that makes you uncomfortable. Moreover, your real name and identity will not be disclosed on public record. As a result, I do not anticipate that there will be any physical or mental discomfort as a result of participating in my study.

POTENTIAL BENEFITS TO SUBJECTS AND/OR TO SOCIETY

Through participating in this study, you will help contribute to our limited knowledge of campus evangelicalism in general and Asian American campus evangelicalism in particular.

PAYMENT FOR PARTICIPATION

There will be no financial payment for participating in the study.

CONFIDENTIALITY

Any information that is obtained in connection with this study and that can be identified with you will remain confidential and will be disclosed only with your permission. Your interview may be audio-taped. However, you have the right to review and if necessary, edit the tapes. Only I will have access to the tapes and they will be erased after my dissertation is completed.

PARTICIPATION AND WITHDRAWAL

You can choose whether to be in this study or not. If you volunteer to be in this study, you may withdraw at any time without consequences of any kind. You may also refuse to answer any questions you don't want to answer and still remain in the study. The investigator may withdraw you from this research if circumstances arise which warrant doing so.

IDENTIFICATION OF INVESTIGATORS

If you have any questions or concerns about the research, please feel free to contact me. My home telephone number is XX and my email address is XX. You can also contact my faculty sponsor, Dr. XX, if you wish. Her campus office number is XX and her email address is XX. You can contact both my faculty sponsor and me at this mailing address: XX-Department of Sociology

RIGHTS OF RESEARCH SUBJECTS

You may withdraw your consent at any time and discontinue participation without penalty. You are not waiving any legal claims, rights, or remedies because of your participation in this research study. If you have questions regarding your rights as a research subject, contact the Office for Protection of Research Subjects XX.

SIGNATURE OF RESEARCH SUBJECT OR LEGAL
REPRESENTATIVE

I understand the procedures described above. My questions have been answered to my satisfaction, and I agree to participate in this study. I have been given a copy of this form.

_____   _____

Name of Subject   Date

SIGNATURE OF INVESTIGATOR (IF REQUIRED BY THE HSPC.)

In my judgment the subject is voluntarily and knowingly giving informed consent and possesses the legal capacity to give informed consent to participate in this research study.

_____   _____

Signature of Investigator   Date

Consent to Participate in Research: Asian American Campus Evangelical Organizations

You are asked to participate in a research study conducted by Rebecca Kim, from the sociology department at the University of XX as part of dissertation research. You were selected as a possible participant in this study because you are a staff and/or a member of a campus evangelical organization and have some knowledge and experience with campus evangelical organizations.

PURPOSE OF THE STUDY

The purpose of the study is to gather general descriptive information on Korean American and other Asian American campus evangelical organizations and find out the major concerns and themes of such organizations. How and why students came to participate in Asian American campus evangelical organizations is also the subject of this study.

PROCEDURES

If you volunteer to participate in this study, I will interview you for approximately 30 minutes to an hour and a half at a location of your choice near campus and ask you questions regarding your involvement in campus ministry.

POTENTIAL RISKS AND DISCOMFORTS

Your participation in this study is voluntary. You may refuse to answer any question that makes you uncomfortable. Moreover, your real name and identity will not be disclosed on public record. As a result, I do not anticipate that there will be any physical or mental discomfort as a result of participating in my study.

POTENTIAL BENEFITS TO SUBJECTS AND/OR TO SOCIETY

Through participating in this study, you will help contribute to our limited knowledge of campus evangelicalism in general and Asian American campus evangelicalism in particular.

PAYMENT FOR PARTICIPATION

There will be no financial payment for participating in the study.

CONFIDENTIALITY

Any information that is obtained in connection with this study and that can be identified with you will remain confidential and will be disclosed only with your permission. Your interview may be audio-taped. However, you have the right to review and if necessary, edit the tapes. Only I will have access to the tapes and they will be erased after my dissertation is completed.

PARTICIPATION AND WITHDRAWAL

You can choose whether to be in this study or not. If you volunteer to be in this study, you may withdraw at any time without consequences of any kind. You may also refuse to answer any questions you don't want to answer and still remain in the study. The investigator may withdraw you from this research if circumstances arise which warrant doing so.

IDENTIFICATION OF INVESTIGATORS

If you have any questions or concerns about the research, please feel free to contact me. My home telephone number is XX and my email address is XX. You can also contact my faculty sponsor, Dr. XX, if you wish. Her campus office number is XX and her email address is XX. You can contact both my faculty sponsor and me at this mailing address:

XX-Department of Sociology

RIGHTS OF RESEARCH SUBJECTS

You may withdraw your consent at any time and discontinue participation without penalty. You are not waiving any legal claims, rights, or remedies because of your participation in this research study. If you have questions regarding your rights as a research subject, contact the Office for Protection of Research Subjects XX.

SIGNATURE OF RESEARCH SUBJECT OR LEGAL REPRESENTATIVE

I understand the procedures described above. My questions have been answered to my satisfaction, and I agree to participate in this study. I have been given a copy of this form.

_____   _____

Name of Subject   Date

SIGNATURE OF INVESTIGATOR (IF REQUIRED BY THE HSPC.)

In my judgment the subject is voluntarily and knowingly giving informed consent and possesses the legal capacity to give informed consent to participate in this research study.

_____   _____

Signature of Investigator   Date

Notes

NOTES TO THE INTRODUCTION

1. These figures for New York City colleges and universities are extrapolated from Sax et al.'s 1997 survey.

2. Asian Americans Changing the Face of Christianity on College Campuses, *Religion News,* February 13, 1999, available at http://www.reporternews.com/999/religion/asian0213.html (accessed 1999).

3. These numbers are applicable for the years 2000 to 2004.

4. Asian American familial cultural backgrounds and group characters can mesh well with conservative Evangelicalism. Evangelicalism's emphasis on hard work, discipline, self-control, and obedience (including its conservative teachings against premarital sex and homosexuality) complement Asian Americans' familial and cultural upbringing and can help them stay on the model minority path of socioeconomic mobility. The Evangelical Christian faith encourages Asian American college students to work hard and live puritanical, disciplined, self-controlled, and obedient lives that "honor one's parents." Through campus ministries, Asian American college students can spend their free time praying, singing praise, and "hanging out" with Christian friends rather than drinking, partying, and exploring alternative lifestyles with their newfound freedom in college.

The image of Jesus who offers unconditional love, forgiveness, and strength to overcome all obstacles (including a difficult chemistry exam) can also appeal to Asian American college students, who experience excessive pressures to succeed. Moreover, being Evangelical Christians can render Asian Americans as less foreign and more American.

5. The second generation is defined as those who are born and raised in the United States with at least one immigrant parent.

6. That is, they comprise at least 90 percent of one racial group.

7. For theologically conservative Evangelical Christians, the literal resurrection of the body and the salvation of the body, mind, and soul are emphasized.

8. "Greek" refers to non-Jews.

9. Originally formulated by Charles Horton Cooley (1909) and used by Milton M. Gordon (1964) in his work on *Assimilation in American Life,* the term

"primary group" is defined as a group that has personal, intimate, and informal, often face-to-face, contact and involves the entire personality of an individual. Primary group relations differ from "secondary group" relations, which are more formal, impersonal, nonintimate, and segmentalized and do not involve the entire personality of an individual (Gordon 1964: 31–32).

10. These numbers are applicable for the fall 1999 semester. Asian Americans include Chinese, Japanese, Korean, Thai/Other Asian, East Indian/Pakistani, Pacific Islander, Vietnamese, and Filipino.

11. I sent a general survey questionnaire via e-mail to all of the members of ACURA and presented my findings at their 2000 annual meeting. The survey asked questions pertaining to the size, growth, ethnic makeup, and variety of ethnic religious organizations on campuses. Ten out of the twenty participants who came to the annual conference responded to the e-mail survey. Most indicated that they witnessed the growth of Asian American campus Evangelical organizations on their university campus and commented on what they felt were factors that contributed to this growth. I was also able to obtain further feedback from the various campus religious organization coordinators at the annual meeting.

12. The organizations have more than thirty regular members and more than five years of history; they are Evangelical Protestant organizations. I categorized an organization as Evangelical Christian if it had the following traits: belief in the sole authority and reliability of the Bible, emphasis on individual faith and salvation of the human soul solely by faith in Jesus Christ, and stress proselytizing nonbelievers. I found out whether an organization identified itself as "Evangelical Christian" or not through the organization's mission statement and by talking to the members and leaders.

13. I am using pseudonyms for the two SGKA campus ministries where I conducted most of my personal interviews.

14. The 1.5 generation were not born in the United States but received their primary education in the United States.

15. Of the fifty Korean American students that I interviewed from the SGKA campus ministries, thirty-eight (76 percent) were U.S.-born, while the rest came to the United States before the age of nine.

NOTES TO CHAPTER I

1. An important factor that made higher education more practical and democratic was the passing of the Morrill Land Grant Act of 1862 and the Morrill Act of 1890.

2. Religion was considered to be part of the "childhood" of the human race, something that humans would naturally grow out of. Many modern social scientists conceded with Anthony F. C. Wallace, a prominent anthropologist of re-

ligion, when he wrote, "the evolutionary future of religion is extinction" (1966: 264).

3. Many religion scholars look on the survival of religion at the voluntary and private group level as an indicator of secularization itself (Chaves 1994). But this is not entirely accurate. Religion may actually become more vibrant precisely because it is no longer institutionalized and has privatized (Warner 1993). With the privatization and marketization of religious organizations, religious organizations will work hard and innovate to satisfy and attract more customers, which can increase individual religious participation.

4. My study focuses on Protestant Christian student organizations on college campuses because such organizations have witnessed the greatest growth in the number of Asian American student members compared with other, more established religious organizations. For example, non-Jews do not usually attend Jewish student organizations, and even Buddhist organizations tend not to be populated by U.S.-born Asian Americans. Christian student organizations also have the longest history on college campuses and are the most numerous.

5. The Bible chair movement ended following a flow of decisions by state and federal courts, as well as states' attorney generals, that removed the legal acceptance of church-supported teaching of religion on public campuses. It was also removed as academia began to regard religion as just another phenomenon in the world that one should test, compare, and study (Butler 1989). Accordingly, Bible chairs were replaced by departments of religion on college and university campuses.

6. Due to the diversity of Evangelicalism and its long history, these figures may differ depending on the sources and definition of Evangelicalism. Finding data on Evangelicalism is also complicated by the fact that it is more of a social movement than a religion and is not tied to a particular denomination.

7. In addition to large interdenominational parachurch Christian campus ministries like IVCF and CCC, which can be found on numerous college and university campuses across the United States, there are Christian campus fellowships that are supported by local churches near campus. Additionally, there are Christian campus fellowships started by students that operate independent of large parachruch organizations, local churches, and denominations.

8. The growth in the number of Asian American Evangelicals is evident in the broader society. But it is most noticeable at the top college and university campuses of America where the concentration of Asian Americans tends to be higher.

9. Figures on the percentages of Korean American students at colleges and universities are hard to come by because most, if not all, schools report aggregate admissions data for Asian Americans and do not distinguish between the different Asian ethnic groups.

10. Students from Asian countries also make up a significant portion of the

foreign student population on many American colleges and universities (Siden 1994).

11. Technically, these pan-ethnic ministries can be referred to as multiethnic ministries since they consist of more than one ethnic group. They can also be referred to as monoracial campus ministries. In this volume, however, I refer to these organizations as pan-ethnic.

12. This was the figure that CCC in Korea provided over the phone in 2000.

13. Available at http://www.kwak.org/kccc/campus.html (accessed March 2006).

14. More recently, KCCC in America has been reaching out to the second generation as well.

15. JEMS is an Evangelical Christian organization that was established following World War II in order to rebuild Japanese American churches and evangelize the Japanese American community, as well as to send missionaries to Japan.

16. *Asian American Christian Fellowship, 25th Anniversary Celebration* (1997: 4–6).

17. Available at http://www.campuscrusadeforchrist.com/aboutus/history/htm. A complete list of the CCC chapters is available on the following website: http://www.uscm.org/locator/index.php (accessed March 14, 2006).

18. Part of the reason the CCC at WU is predominately white is because there is a separate Asian American CCC, called Epic, which is also on the WU campus. Asian American students who come to CCC are encouraged to go to Epic instead. Because Epic is relatively new and only has a few members, I chose AACF, instead of Epic, as one of my six main case studies.

19. However, this is how the head staff of WU CCC described the South Asian American staff: "One of our leader staff is Indian; he converted from Hinduism, . . . but he is as white as can be."

NOTES TO CHAPTER 2

1. Hawaii officially became a U.S. territory on February 22, 1900, and it became the fiftieth state of the Union on August 21, 1959.

2. Today's Korean churches in America, however, are not known for their political activism.

3. The story of Syngman Rhee, the first president of the Republic of Korea after Korea gained independence from Japan in 1945, captures this well. Before he became the president of Korea, Rhee was first a labor immigrant to Hawaii in 1905. He formed the Korean Independence Church of Hawaii and was a pastor for Korean Americans during the 1920s.

4. Many of the Korean wives of American GIs, however, took a significant

role in sponsoring their relatives from Korea to bring them to the United States with the passage of the Immigration Act of 1965 (Kwon et al. 2001).

5. It has also been argued that part of the reason that Christianity took root in Korea was the ability of Christian missionaries to fuse traditional Korean culture with Christian theology. For example, to make Protestant Christianity more appealing to the Korean people, Christianity for Koreans have "shamanized," emphasizing the magical, spiritual, and this-worldly rewards (Clark 1986; A. Kim 2000). The fact that Korean Protestantism adopted the primitive and revered Korean concept of *Hananim* as the word for the Christian God also made Christianity more attractive to Koreans. This, along with traditional characterizations of *Hananim* as omniscient, omnipotent, sympathetic to human suffering, and the creator of the world, made the imported Protestant image of God fit well with Koreans' preexisting notions of a supreme deity. This kind of syncretism made Protestant Christianity more amenable to Koreans.

6. Of course, part of the reason for their exit is that they are "in college" or are busy pursuing their careers in other parts of the country and cannot practically continue to go to the same church. Nevertheless, they tend not to attend a church similar to their parents' immigrant church once they are settled.

7. Pearl Jam is an American "grunge" rock band.

8. The existence of an immigration law which makes any alien minister serving at least thirty church members eligible for permanent residence in the United States contributes to schisms within the immigrant church. An assistant minister can take several members of a church and break away to start another church to gain permanent residence in the United States (Alumkal 2003; I. Kim 1981). Additionally, the importance of the ethnic church for congregants' sense of prestige and status, as well as the disproportionate number of actively engaged lay leaders within the immigrant church, makes schisms more likely. The fact that there are many alternative congregations that Korean immigrants can attend also makes conflict and "church-hopping" more common.

9. However, many SGKAs fail to understand that Korean immigrant churches in the United States were not established for simply "biblical" reasons in the first place. Instead, they were founded in part because the Korean community was in great need of social institutions that provide fellowship, maintain homeland traditions, offer social services, and sustain social positions. Korean immigrant churches aim to preserve Korean culture and identity while serving as the most central social institution in the ethnic community for meeting the pressing needs of immigrants struggling to establish themselves in their new homeland. Thus, if there is much splitting and struggles over power, status, and positions, it is because there are so many lay leaders who are involved in immigrant churches. And the reason there are so many lay leaders is because immigrants cannot attain their preimmigrant levels of status and respect in their new host

society. Consequently, ethnic churches serve as the institutions through which immigrants can regain and reclaim their preimmigrant status. Making matters more difficult for the first generation are their language and cultural barriers, which, in turn, prevent them from reaching out to the broader, non-Korean community. Like most immigrants, first-generation Koreans are also most concerned about the future financial stability of their families and children and, as a result, tend to be more pragmatic than the second generation regarding their religious orientation and practices. They thus tend to push their children to focus on educational and professional achievements over purely religious pursuits.

NOTES TO CHAPTER 3

1. While everyone has equal access, most students do not go to a campus ministry alone. They find their way to campus ministries because friend(s), roommate(s), classmate(s), or someone else personally invited them. In the beginning of the school year, students may also "check out" and "shop around" for a campus ministry with their friends. Few venture into a campus ministry by themselves. Not surprisingly, one of the common questions that newcomers of campus ministries are asked is "Who did you come with?" or "Who brought you?"

2. In the past, they had several black students lead the praise, which IVCF staff members noted led to a different kind of "gospel" style of praise that made some white students uncomfortable. In the times that I have participated in the IVCF weekly gatherings, however, the praise was consistently led by a white man with a racially diverse band.

3. "God" and "Jesus" are commonly used interchangeably by campus Evangelicals.

4. Quiet time is personal fellowship time with God/Jesus—praying, reading, and reflecting on "God's words" in the Bible.

5. Unlike KAMC, CSF does not have a regular pastor who comes to speak. Instead, the director of CSF, a faculty member of a local seminary and pastor of a Korean American church, invites various Korean American as well as non–Korean American pastors that he knows to come and speak at CSF.

6. Pastor Peter is an SGKA who graduated from an American seminary and leads a local SGKA-based church. He volunteers his services for KAMC by providing overall leadership for the elected five "core" student members who lead KAMC.

7. One may occasionally hear members of SGKA campus ministries, particularly KAMC, using deferential Korean terms, honorifics, to address elders and senior leaders, but this is relatively rare.

8. This kind of prayer, however, is a contested practice. Some Korean American Christians argue that it is "too emotional"; others argue that it is mechanical or perfunctory (Yoon 2005: 167–168).

1. Although this kind of ethnic density is relatively uncommon, it can be found at other universities, high schools, and junior high schools in many large cities (Logan et al. 2001).

2. Having experienced their religious participation with other SGKAs, SGKAs also tend to have more information and social ties that lead them to other co-ethnic campus ministries, as a student explains: "It was just more comfortable . . . I just knew more people there and heard more about it than the other Christian fellowships." In many cases, Korean Americans note how older "brothers" or "sisters" or friends from their church told them about a Korean American campus ministry long before they attended college and encouraged them to join. An SGKA recalls how his former Bible study teacher from church influenced his decision to attend CSF:

I know this guy Joe. He was the president of Christian Student Fellowship [CSF] couple of years back. . . . He was my Bible study teacher (at church). He went to a church in the valley when I was like in tenth grade. He went to medical school but still kept in contact with me. And he introduced me to John and Mike at this event where upperclassmen met up with incoming people and from then it was like, yeah, CSF.

Many Korean American students thus join a Korean American campus ministry because they know people who were or are currently attending the campus ministry and are more familiar with them. Some students decide to attend a Korean American campus ministry even though they initially found other non–Korean American campus ministries more appealing. An SGKA recalls her experience as a freshman trying to decide which organization she wanted to regularly attend: "Actually I wanted to go to IV[CF], but I did not know as many people there . . . but I knew people at KAMC." Thus, having previous social ties with people that they are already familiar with is important.

Because Korean American students are likely to have social ties with the larger Korean Christian community, they also have more information on Korean American campus ministries than on other campus ministries. Through the available Korean Christian networks, SGKAs are more likely to know when and where Korean American campus ministries meet and what sort of activities they have than they are about non-Korean campus ministries. A student explains why he chose to attend a Korean American campus ministry: "Why did I choose KAMC? I did not hear about the other ones too much. . . . Like I kind of saw the groups out there, but I did not put the effort to try it out. I guess I would have tried it out if I did not know anything at first, but because I knew what KAMC was like before, I did not really bother." Thus, pursuing what is most familiar and similar also means that individuals will follow those social ties and information flows that come to them most readily and easily.

NOTES TO CHAPTER 5

1. Asian Americans began modifying mostly Japanese imports in the 1990s with spoilers, large exhaust tips, racing rims, uni-blade windshield wipers, driving lights, performance seat covers, stickers, and 130-pulse decibel stereo systems. To increase torque and horsepower, the cars were also lowered, suspensions and exhausts were added, and nitrous oxide–injected engines were installed. They look like race cars and often have Japanese characters written on them.

2. As an SGKA explains:
When you think of Korean guys now, there are different categories. You have got the Asian guy that has a fixed up Prelude or Accord; . . . they like to go out and have a lot of parties and such. They are always cursing, smoking, spitting, and hanging out. They have this whole pride thing going on; . . . they are elitist and exclusive. Then you have another group; . . . they are not like that. They could do that too, but they are not so bad.

3. In 1982, a Chinese American man named Vincent Chin was killed in Detroit, Michigan, by two white autoworkers who mistook him for a Japanese man. As a young draftsman, Vincent Chin was attending a bachelor party at a strip club when a white autoworker insulted Chin across the bar yelling, "It's because of you little motherfuckers that we're out of work" and referred to Chin as a "chink," "nip," and "jap." This then led to an altercation that included another autoworker, who had recently been laid off from his job at an auto plant. The two autoworkers blamed the Japanese for the ailing U.S. auto industry and their job loss and took it out on a Chinese American man who looked Japanese in their eyes. After the altercation broke off, the two white autoworkers caught up with Chin and beat him with a baseball bat, which eventually led to Chin's death four days later (five days before his wedding). In the end, neither of the two autoworkers served a jail sentence; they had to pay a $3,700 fine and were put on two years probation.

In 1999, Dr. Wen Ho Lee, a Chinese American scientist and a naturalized U.S. citizen, was accused of stealing U.S. nuclear secrets and giving them to the People's Republic of China (PRC). He was thus terminated from his job (just nine months short of retirement) and was incarcerated for nine months. He was denied bail, put in shackles, and placed in solitary confinement. It was later determined that the specific data the PRC had obtained could not have come from the lab where Dr. Lee worked and that such information would not have been ascertainable by someone with Dr. Lee's knowledge.

In the 1970s and early 1980s, the entry of Vietnamese people into the fishing industry of the Gulf Coast sparked resentment from native-born fishermen who felt threatened by the competition. In 1983 in Davis, California, a Vietnamese high school student was taunted by several white high school students and later stabbed to death. Six year later in Raleigh, North Carolina, a Chinese American was beaten to death by men who were angry over the Vietnam War. The men mistook the Chinese American for a Vietnamese. A year later, a Vietnamese American was stomped to death by skinheads in Houston, Texas.

4. Available at http://www.census.gov/Press-Release/www/releases/archives/income_wealth/002484.html (accessed March 2006).

5. There are also noticeable socioeconomic status differences across Asian American groups. According to the 2000 U.S. Census, 42.7 percent of Asian Americans aged 25 and over had bachelor's degrees or higher compared with 22.8 percent of the total U.S. population. Breaking the different Asian ethnic groups down, 60.9 percent of Asian Indians aged 25 and over had bachelor's degrees or higher compared with 46.6 percent of Chinese, 19.5 percent of Vietnamese, and 9.1 percent of Cambodian Americans aged 25 and over. Moreover, 12.4 percent of the total U.S. population lived under the federal poverty level, compared with 12.6 percent of Asian Americans overall and 13.2 percent Chinese, 9.2 percent Japanese, 16.0 percent Vietnamese, and 29.3 percent Cambodians.

6. U.S. Census Bureau, Annual Demographic Supplement to the March 2002 current population survey.

7. The model minority stereotype also pits Asian Americans against other minorities. The argument is as follows: If Asian Americans can make it despite obstacles of discrimination, why can't the blacks and Hispanics? The model image divides racial minorities into the good and deserving "model" minority versus the undeserving minority and excuses the white majority from confronting problems of racism and discrimination. Relatedly, the model minority image upholds the classic model of American success—that anyone can make it in America if only they try hard enough, which can further legitimate the absence of efforts to address racial inequality (Kibria 2002; Osajima 1988; Woo 2000). Furthermore, the perceptions of Asian Americans as successful discourage Asian Americans from being politically engaged and make them less likely to seek out public assistance and turn to mental health care services for help.

8. There are cultural troupes like *HanNuRi,* which fosters cultural awareness among Korean Americans in California. Similar cultural organizations that aim to nurture a sense of Korean heritage and identity among SGKAs can also be found in major cities like New York and Philadelphia.

NOTES TO CHAPTER 6

1. The name of the campus ministry has been changed for this study.

2. A Korean American student notes how he is often singled out by the Asian American campus groups when he is with his white friends: "When I am walking [on the popular walkway on campus where the various student groups

gather], I noticed that I would get the various flyers from the Asian [Christian] groups, but my white friends would not."

3. Although I did not find any SGKAs in the white CCC, I interviewed an SGKA who participated in another predominately white campus ministry and another Korean American who attended a predominately white church near WU. I also interviewed two other SGKA students who had previously attended a white campus ministry and a white church but now attend a Korean American campus ministry and church.

4. Similarly, those who have co-ethnic ties can later cross ethnic group boundaries at the primary group level.

NOTES TO CHAPTER 7

1. Tensions can also exist between Asian American ethnic and religious identities because Christianity can be viewed as a "white man's religion." However, because Korea had a relatively positive historical relationship with Christian missionaries and has more than a quarter of its current population identifying itself as Christian, most Korean Americans did not view their Christian religion as a "white man's religion."

2. The idea that religion can provide man with a sense of community and place originates from the work of Emile Durkheim, who argued that religion is essentially society worshipping itself: "The sacred principle is nothing more nor less than society transfigured and personified. . . . The individual gets from society the best part of himself, all that gives him a distinct character and a special place" (1995: 347). While Durkheim's conceptualization of religion, equating religion to society, has caused much controversy and debate, Durkheim's insight into the intimate relationship between religion and man's belonging to society remains. Religion may not be society, but religion provides an important basis for social unity and the sense of belonging.

3. According to the rational choice theory of religion (or the religious economies theory), religious pluralism is good for religious consumption. Contrary to the pronouncement that religion will disappear or decline with modernization and increasing pluralism, the religious economies model argues that religious participation actually increases in pluralistic modern societies. A religious market characterized by pluralism rather than a monopoly heightens religious participation because it is precisely through a variety of religious groups that the divergent interests and needs of a pluralistic society are met (Finke and Stark 1992; Iannaccone 1990, 1995; Stark and Iannaccone 1993; Warner 1993). Pluralistic competition in modern societies forces religious "firms" to "produce efficiently a wide range of alternative faiths well adapted to the needs of consumers" (Iannaccone 1992: 128). This then increases religious consumption by

individuals who rationally evaluate the costs and benefits of the goods available in the market based on their specific needs and preferences.

The rational choice theory of religion is not without criticisms. The data that religious economies theorists have used to support rational choice theory's predictions have been challenged (Bruce 1993, 1995). It has also been argued that individuals do not always maximize benefits and minimize costs, particularly with something like religion, which has traditionally been thought of as irrational in and of itself (Bruce 1993; Etzioni 1988; Ferree 1992).

In regard to campus Evangelicals and the religious marketplace, I am not trying to argue that Evangelicalism itself is more vital because America is a religiously plural versus a monopolistic society. People are not more "religious" simply because there are competing faiths. However, I argue that having various competitive religious firms within a particular religious tradition does provide religious consumers of that faith more choices and therefore can increase the likelihood that they would take part in a religious community. And I argue that, given the cultural and structural constraints and the available information regarding the variety of campus ministries, campus Evangelicals will choose a religious community that will offer them the most personal benefits and comforts. They will choose a campus ministry that can offer ethnic as well as religious goods.

4. Additional information can be found at http://www.veritas.org/index.html (accessed March 14, 2006).

5. These rationalizations suggest that those who are more religious would be able to overcome such inconsistencies and have more integrated religious organizations. Interestingly, the most diverse Christian groups on campus were those that were labeled "cultic" and considered religiously extremist.

NOTES TO THE CONCLUSION

1. In addition, the co-ethnic ties that SGKAs make during their college years tend to form the nucleus of their close ties after college. Voluntary ethnic associations also continue to form in every major profession (e.g., law, medicine, and academia).

2. Indeed, SGKAs commonly travel to Korea during the summers to connect with relatives and learn more about their Korean heritage, culture, and language.

3. I assume that they not only have these choices but also are conscious of them.

References

Abelmann, Nancy, and John Lie. 1995. *Blue Dreams: Korean Americans and the Los Angeles Riots.* Cambridge: Harvard University Press.

Abramson, Harold J. 1973. *Ethnic Diversity in Catholic America.* New York: Wiley.

Alba, Richard, and Victor Nee. 1996. The Assimilation of Immigrant Groups: Concept, Theory, and Evidence. Paper presented at the Conference on Becoming American/American Becoming: International Migration to the United States. Social Science Research Council, Sanibel, Fl., January 18–21.

———. 2003. *Remaking the American Mainstream: Assimilation and Contemporary Immigration.* Cambridge: Harvard University Press.

Alumkal, Antony. 2001. Being Korean, Being Christian: Particularlism and Universalism in a Second-Generation Congregation. Pp. 181–192 in Ho-Youn Kwon, Kwang Chung Kim, and R. Stephen Warner (eds.), *Korean Americans and Their Religions: Pilgrims and Missionaries from a Different Shore.* University Park: Pennsylvania State University Press.

———. 2002. Race in American Evangelicalism: A Racial Formation Analysis. Paper presented at the American Sociological Association, Chicago, August 18.

———. 2003. *Asian American Evangelical Churches: Race, Ethnicity, and Assimilation in the Second Generation.* New York: LFB Scholarly Publishing.

Anderson, David A. 2004. *Multicultural Ministry: Finding Your Church's Unique Rhythm.* Grand Rapids, MI: Zondervan.

Asian American Christian Fellowship, 25th Anniversary Celebration. Los Angeles: Asian American Christian Fellowship, 1997.

Bankston, Carl L. III, and Min Zhou. 1995. Religious Participation, Ethnic Identification, and Adaptation of Vietnamese Adolescents in an Immigrant Community. *Sociological Quarterly* 36: 523–534.

Barnes, Jessica S., and Claudette E. Bennett. 2002. *The Asian Population: 2000.* Census 2000 Brief. Washington, D.C.: U.S. Census Bureau. Available at http://www.census.gov/prod/2002pubs/C2Kbr01_16.pdf (accessed April 5, 2006).

Bell, Daniel. 1975. Ethnicity and Social Change. Pp. 141–176 in Nathan Glazer and Daniel P. Moynihan (eds.), *Ethnicity: Theory and Experience.* Cambridge: Harvard University Press.

Bellah, Robert N. 1970. *Beyond Belief: Essays on Religion in a Post-Traditional World*. Berkeley: University of California Press.

Berger, Peter L. 1967. *The Sacred Canopy*. Garden City, N.Y.: Doubleday.

Bramadat, Paul A. 2000. *The Church on the World's Turf: An Evangelical Christian Group at a Secular University*. Oxford: Oxford University Press.

Brubaker, Rogers. 2001. The Return of Assimilation? Changing Perspectives on Immigration and Its Sequels in France, Germany, and the United States. *Ethnic and Racial Studies* 24: 531–548.

Bruce, Steve. 1993. Religion and Rational Choice: A Critique of Economic Explanations of Religious Behavior. *Sociology of Religion* 54 (2): 193–205.

———. 1995. The Truth about Religion in Britain. *Journal for the Scientific Study of Religion* 34: 417–430.

Burtchaell, James Tunstead. 1998. *The Dying of the Light: The Disengagement of Colleges and Universities from their Christian Churches*. Cambridge: Wm. B. Erdmans Publishing.

Busto, Rudy V. 1996. The Gospel According to the Model Minority? *Amerasia Journal* 22: 133–147.

Butler, John. 1989. *Religion on Campus*. San Francisco: Jossey-Bass.

Calderon, Jose. 1992. "Hispanic" and "Latino": The Viability of Categories for Panethnic Studies. *Latin American Perspectives* 19 (4): 37–44.

Carnes, Tony, and Fenggang Yang, 2004. *Asian American Religions: Making and Remaking of Borders and Boundaries*. New York: New York University Press.

Cha, Peter. 2001. Ethnic Identity Formation and Participation in Immigrant Churches: Second-Generation Korean American Experience. Pp. 141–156 in Ho-Youn Kwon, Kwang Chung Kim, and R. Stephen Warner (eds.), *Korean Americans and Their Religions: Pilgrims and Missionaries from a Different Shore*. University Park: Pennsylvania State University Press.

Chai, Karen. 1998. Competing for the Second Generation: English-Language Ministry at a Korean Protestant Church. Pp. 295–331 in R. Stephen Warner and Judith G. Wittner (eds.), *Gatherings in Diaspora: Religious Communities and the New Immigration*. Philadelphia: Temple University Press.

———. 2001. Beyond "Strictness" to Distinctiveness: Generational Transition in Koreap Protestant Churches. Pp. 157–180 in Ho-youn Kwon, Kwang Chung Kim, and R. Stephen Warner (eds.), *Korean Americans and Their Religions: Pilgrims and Missionaries from a Different Shore*. University Park: Pennsylvania State University Press.

Chan, Sucheng. 1991. *Asian Americans: An Interpretive History*. New York: Twayne Publishers.

Chang, Carrie. 2000. Amen. Pass the Kimchee: Why Are Asian Americans on College Converting to Christianity in Droves? *Monolid: An Asian American Magazine for Those Who Aren't Blinking*. 1 (1): 1–9. Available at http://www.monolid.com/articles1.html.

Chaves, Mark. 1994. Secularization as Declining Religious Authority. *Social Forces* 72: 749–774.

———. 1999. National Congregations Study. Unpublished ms. Department of Sociology, University of Arizona.

Cheng, Lucie, and Philip Q. Yang. 1996. Asians: The "Model Minority" Deconstructed. Pp. 305–344 in Roger Waldinger and Mehdi Bozorgmehr (eds.), *Ethnic Los Angeles*. New York: Russell Sage Foundation.

Cherry, Conrad, Betty A. DeBerg, and Amanda Porterfield. 2001. *Religion on Campus*. Chapel Hill: North Carolina University Press.

Cho, San Oak. 1984. A Study of Korean American Churches and Their Growth in the U.S. Ph.D. dissertation, Fuller Theological Seminary, Pasadena, California.

Chong, Kelly H. 1998. What It Means to Be Christian: The Role of Religion in the Construction of Ethnic Identity and Boundary among Second Generation Korean Americans. *Sociology of Religion* 59: 259–286.

Choy, Bong-Youn. 1979. *Koreans in America*. Chicago: Nelson-Hall.

Clark, Donald N. 1986. *Christianity in Modern Korea*. Boston: University Press of America.

Conzen, Kathleen Neils, David A. Gerber, Ewa Morawska, George E. Pozzetta, and Rudolph J. Vecoli. 1992. The Invention of Ethnicity: A Perspective from the U.S.A. *Journal of American Ethnic History* 11: 3–41.

Cooley, Charles Horton. 1909. *Social Organization*. New York: Scribner's.

DeYoung, Curtiss Paul, Michael O. Emerson, George Yancey, and Karen Chai Kim. 2003. *United by Faith: The Multi-racial Congregation*. Oxford: Oxford University Press.

DeYoung, Curtiss Paul, Michael O. Emerson, George Yancey, and Karen Chai Kim. 2005. All Churches Should Be Multiracial: The Biblical Case. *Christianity Today* April: 32–35.

Duncan, Otis Dudley, David L. Featherman, and Beverly Duncan. 1972. *Socioeconomic Background and Achievement*. New York: Seminar.

Durkheim, Emile. 1995. *Elementary Forms of the Religious Life*. New York: Free Press. Originally published 1915.

Emerson, Michael O., and Christian Smith. 2000. *Divided by Faith*. Oxford: Oxford University Press.

Etzioni, Amitai. 1988. *The Moral Dimension: Toward a New Economics*. New York: Free Press.

Ferree, Myra Marx. 1992. The Political Context of Rationality: Rational Choice Theory and Resource Mobilization. Pp. 29–52 in Aldon D. Morris and Carol McClurg Mueller (eds.), *Frontiers in Social Movement Theory*. New Haven: Yale University Press.

Finke, Roger, and Rodney Stark. 1992. *The Churching of America 1776–1990*. New Brunswick, N.J.: Rutgers University Press.

Gallup, George Jr., and D. Michael Lindsay. 1999. *Surveying the Religious Landscape*. Harrisburg, Pa.: Morehouse Publishing.

Gans, Herbert. 1979. Symbolic Ethnicity: The Future of Ethnic Groups and Cultures in America. *Ethnic and Racial Studies* 2: 1–20.

———. 1992. Second Generation Decline: Scenarios for the Economic and Ethnic Futures of the Post-1965 American Immigrants. *Ethnic and Racial Studies* 15: 173–192.

Gibson, Margaret. A. 1988. *Accommodation without Assimilation*. Ithaca: Cornell University Press.

Glazer, Nathan, and Daniel P. Moynihan. 1975. *Beyond the Melting Pot*. Cambridge: Massachusetts Institute of Technology Press.

Goette, Robert D. 1993. The Transformation of a First-Generation Church into a Bilingual Second-Generation Church. Pp. 237–251 in Ho-Youn Kwon and Shim Kim (eds.), *The Emerging Generation of Korean Americans*. Seoul: Kyung Hee University Press.

Gordon, Milton M. 1964. *Assimilation in American Life*. New York: Oxford University Press.

Greeley, Andrew M. 1972. *The Denominational Society*. Glenview: Scott, Foresman.

———. 1974. *Ethnicity in the United States*. New York: Wiley.

Guillermo, Artemio. 1991. *Churches Aflame: Asian Americans and United Methodism*. Nashville: Abingdon.

Haller, Mark H. 1973. Recurring Themes. Pp. 277–291 in Allen F. Davis and Mark Haller (eds.), *The Peoples of Philadelphia*. Philadelphia: Temple University Press.

Handlin, Oscar. 1951. *The Uprooted*. Boston: Little, Brown.

Herberg, Will. 1955. *Protestant, Catholic, Jew*. New York: Doubleday.

Hofstadter, Richard, and C. De Witt Hardy. 1952. *The Development and Scope of Higher Education in the United States*. New York: Columbia University Press.

Hong, Peter Y. 2000. The Changing Face of Higher Education in America. Available at http://www.aac.sunysb.edu/asianamericanstudies/changingface.htr (accessed June 2001).

Hsia, Jayjia, and Marsha Hirano-Nakanishi. 1989. The Demographics of Diversity: Asian Americans and Higher Education. *Change: The Magazine of Higher Learning* November/December: 20.

Hu-Dehart, Evelyn. 1994. P. C. and the Politics of Multiculturalism in Higher Education. Pp. 242–256 in Steven Gregory and Roger Sanjek (eds.), *Race*. New Brunswick, N.J.: Rutgers University Press.

Hune, Shirley. 1989. Opening the American Mind and Body: The Role of Asian American Studies. *Change: The Magazine of Higher Learning* November/December: 59.

Hunter, James. 1983. *American Evangelicalism: Conservative Religion and the Quandary of Modernity.* New Brunswick, N.J.: Rutgers University Press.

———. 1987. *Evangelicalism: The Coming Generation.* Chicago: University of Chicago Press.

Hurh, Won Moo, and Kwang Chung Kim. 1984. *Korean Immigrants in America: A Structural Analysis of Ethnic Confinement and Adhesive Adaptation.* Madison, N.J.: Fairleigh Dickenson University Press.

———. 1990. Religious Participation of Korean Immigrants in the United States. *Journal for the Scientific Study of Religion* 29: 19–34.

Iannaccone, Laurence R. 1990. Religious Practice: A Human Capital Approach. *Journal for the Scientific Study of Religion* 29: 297–314.

———. 1992. Religious Markets and the Economics of Religion. *Social Compass* 39: 123–131.

———. 1995. Voodoo Economics? Reviewing the Rational Choice Approach to Religion. *Journal for the Scientific Study of Religion* 34: 76–88.

Jeung, Russell. 2000. A New People Coming Together: Asian American Pan-ethnic Congregations. Ph.D. dissertation, University of California, Berkeley.

———. 2002. Asian American Pan-ethnic Formation and Congregational Culture. Pp. 215–244 in Pyong Gap Min and Jung Ha Kim (eds.), *Religions in Asian America: Building Faith Communities.* Walnut Creek, Calif.: AltaMira Press.

———. 2005. *Faithful Generations: Race and New Asian American Churches.* Brunswick, N.J.: Rutgers University Press.

Johnstone, Ronald L. 2001. *Religion in Society: A Sociology of Religion.* Upper Saddle River, N.J.: Prentice Hall.

Kibria, Nazli. 2002. *Becoming Asian American: Second-Generation Chinese and Korean American Identities.* Baltimore: Johns Hopkins University Press.

Kim, Andrew Eungi. 2000. Christianity, Shamanism, and Modernization in South Korea. *Cross Currents* 50 (1–2): 112–119,

Kim, David Kyuman. 1993. Becoming: Korean Americans, Faith, and Identity: Observations on an Emerging Culture. M.Div. thesis, Harvard Divinity School, Cambridge.

Kim, Ilpyong J. 2004. *Korean Americans: Past, Present, and Future.* Elizabeth, N.J.: Hollym International.

Kim, Ilsoo. 1981. *New Urban Immigrants: The Korean Community in New York.* Princeton, N.J.: Princeton University Press.

Kim, Jung Ha. 2002. Cartography of Korean American Protestant Faith Communities in the United States. Pp. 185–214 in Pyong Gap Min and Jung Ha Kim (eds.), *Religions in Asian America: Building Faith Communities.* Walnut Creek, Calif.: AltaMira Press.

Kim, Kwang Chung, and Shin Kim. 1996. Ethnic Meanings of Korean Immigrant Churches. Paper presented at the Sixty North Park College Korean Symposium, Chicago, October 12.

Kim, Kwang Chung, and Shin Kim. 2001. Ethnic Roles of Korean Immigrant churches in the United States. Pp. 71–94 in Ho-Youn Kwon, Kwong Chung Kim, and R. Stephen Warner (eds.), *Korean Americans and Their Religions: Pilgrims and Missionaries from a Different Shore*. University Park: Pennsylvania State University Press.

Kim, Rebecca. 2004. Asian American College Campus Evangelicals: Constructing and Negotiating Ethnic and Religious Boundaries. Pp. 141–159 in Tony Carnes and Fenggang Yang (eds.), *Asian American Religion: The Making and Remaking of Borders and Boundaries*. New York: New York University Press.

Kim, Won Moo, and Kwang Chung Kim. 1990. Religious Participation of Korean Immigrants in the United States. *Journal for the Scientific Study of Religion* 29: 19–34.

Kristof, Nicholas D. 2003. God, Satan, and the Media. *New York Times*, March 4, Sec. A, P. 25, Col. 6.

Kwon, Ho-Youn, Kwang Chung Kim, and R. Stephen Warner. 2001. *Korean Americans and Their Religions: Pilgrims and Missionaries from a Different Shore*. University Park: Penn State University Press.

Kwon, Victoria Hyonchu, Helen Rose Ebaugh, and Jacqueline Hagan. 1997. The Structure and Functions of Cell Group Ministry in a Korean Christian Church. *Journal for the Scientific Study of Religion* 36: 247–256.

Lee, Jennifer, and Frank D. Bean. 2003. Beyond Black and White: Remaking Race in America. *Contexts* 2(3): 26–33.

———. 2004. America's Changing Color Lines: Immigration, Race/Ethnicity, and Multiracial Identification. *Annual Review of Sociology* 30: 221–242.

Lee, Jennifer, and Min Zhou. 2004. *Asian American Youth: Culture,Identity, and Ethnicity*. New York: Routledge.

Lee, Robert G. 1999. *Orientals*. Philadelphia: Temple University Press.

Logan, John. 2001. *The New Ethnic Enclaves in America's Suburbs*. Report by the Lewis Mumford Center, July 9. Available at http://mumford.albany.edu/census/suburban/Suburban Reort/page1.html (accessed March 15, 2006).

Logan, John, Dierdre Oakley, Polly Smith, Jacob Stowell, and Brian Stults. 2001. *Separating the Children*. Report by the Lewis Mumford Center, May 4. Available at http://mumford.albany.edu/census/Under18Pop/U18Preport/page1.html (accessed March 15, 2006).

Lopez, David, and Yen Espiritu. 1990. Panethnicity in the United States: A Theoretical Framework. *Ethnic and Racial Studies* 13: 198–224.

Malinowski, Bronislaw. 1954. *Magic, Science and Religion*. Garden City, N.Y.: Doubleday. Originally published in 1925.

Marsden, George M. 1994. *The Soul of the American University: From Protestant Establishment to Established Nonbelief.* Oxford: Oxford University Press.

Marsden, Peter V. 1987. Core Discussion Networks of Americans. *American Sociological Review* 52: 122–313.

McCormick, Thomas R. 1987. *Campus Ministry in the Coming Age.* St. Louis, Mo.: CBP Press.

McPherson, Miller, Lynn Smith-Lovin, and James M. Cook. 2001. Birds of a Feather: Homophily in Social Networks. *Annual Review Sociology* 27: 415–444.

Min, Pyong Gap. 1992. The Structure and Social Functions of Korean Immigrant Churches in the United States. *International Migration Review* 26: 1370–1394.

———. 1999. A Comparison of Post-1965 and Turn-of-the-Century Immigrants. *Journal of American Ethnic History* 18: 65–94.

———. 2000. Immigrants' Religion and Ethnicity: A Comparison of Indian Hindu and Korean Christian Immigrants in the United States. *Bulletin of the Royal Institute of Inter-Faith Studies* 2: 122–140.

———. 2002. *The Second Generation: Ethnic Identity among Asian Americans.* Walnut Creek, Calif.: AltaMira Press.

Nagel, Joane. 1986. The Political Construction of Ethnicity. Pp. 93–112 in Susan Olzak and Joane Nagel (eds.), *Competitive Ethnic Relations.* Orlando, Fl.: Academic Press.

Nakanishi, Don. 1995. A Quota on Excellence? The Asian American Admissions Debate. Pp. 273–284 in Don Nakanishi and Tina Nishida (eds.), *The Asian Pacific American Educational Experience: A Sourcebook for Teachers and Students.* New York: Routledge.

Niebuhr, H. Richard. 1929. *Social Sources of Denominationalism.* New York: H. Holt.

Okamoto, Kina. 2003. Toward a Theory of Panethnicity: Explaining Asian American Collective Action. *American Sociological Review* 68 (6): 811–842.

Okihiro, Gary Y. 1994. *Margins and Mainstreams: Asians in American History and Culture.* Seattle: University of Washington Press.

Osajima, Keith. 1988. Asian Americans as the Model Minority: An Analysis of Popular Press Images in the 1960's and 1980's. Pp. 165–174 in Gary Y. Okihiro, Shirley Hune, Arthur A. Hansen, and John M. Liu (eds.), *Reflections on Shattered Windows: Promises and Prospects of Asian American Studies.* Pullman: Washington State University Press.

Pai, Young, Delores Pemberton, and John Worley. 1987. *Findings on Korean American Early Adolescents.* Kansas City: University of Missouri School of Education.

Park, Kyeyoung. 1997. *The Korean American Dream: Immigrants and Small Businesses in New York City.* Ithaca: Cornell University Press.

Park, Robert E. 1950. *Race and Culture.* Glencoe, Ill.: Free Press. Originally published in 1926.

Park, Robert E., and Ernest W. Burgess. 1921. *Introduction to the Science of Sociology.* Chicago: University of Chicago Press.

Portes, Alejandro, and Robert L. Bach. 1985. *Latin Journey: Cuban and Mexican Immigrants in the United States.* Berkeley: University of California Press.

Portes, Alejandro, and Min Zhou. 1993. The New Second Generation: Segmented Assimilation and Its Variants. *Annals of the American Academy of Political and Social Science* 530: 74–96.

Quebedeaux, Richard. 1974. *The Young Evangelicals.* New York: Harper and Row.

Reeves, Terrance J., and Claudette E. Bennett. 2004. *We the People: Asians in the United States.* Census 2000 Special Reports. Washington, D.C.: U.S. Census Bureau. Available at http://www.census.gov/prod/2004pubs/censr_17.pdf (accessed April 5, 2006).

Rumbaut, Rubén G., and Alejandro Portes. 2001. *Ethnicities: Children of Immigrants in America.* Berkeley: University of California Press.

Sax, Linda J., Alexander W. Astin, William S. Korn, and K. M. Mahoney. 1997. *The American Freshman: National Norms for Fall 1997.* Los Angeles: Higher Education Research Institute, Graduate School of Education and Information Studies, UCLA.

Shockley, Donald G. 1989. *Campus Ministry: The Church beyond Itself.* Louisville, Ky.: Westminster/John Knox.

Siden, Ruth. 1994. *Battling Bias: The Struggle for Identity and Community on College Campuses.* New York: Penguin.

Sloan, Douglas. 1994. *Faith and Knowledge: Mainline Protestantism and American Higher Education.* Louisville, Ky.: Westminster/John Knox.

Smith, Timothy L. 1978. Religion and Ethnicity in America. *American Historical Review* 83: 1155–1185.

Sollors, Werner. 1991. *The Invention of Ethnicity.* Oxford: Oxford University Press.

Song, Minho. 1994. Towards the Successful Movement of the English-Speaking Ministry within the Korean Immigrant Church. Paper presented at Katalyst, Sandy Cove, Md., March 21–24.

Stark, Rodney, and Laurence R. Iannaccone. 1993. Rational Choice Propositions about Religious Movements. *Religion and the Social Order* 3A: 241–261.

Takagi, Dana Y. 1992. *The Retreat from Race: Asian American Admissions and Racial Politics.* New Brunswick, N.J.: Rutgers University Press.

Takagi, Ronald. 1993. *A Different Mirror: A History of Multicultural America.* Boston: Little, Brown.

Tokunaga, Paul. 2003. *Invitation to Lead: Guidance for Emerging Asian American Leaders.* Downers Grove, Ill.: InterVarsity Press.

Tseng, Timothy. 2002. Second-Generation Chinese Evangelical Use of the Bible in Identity Discourse in North America. *Semeia: The Bible in Asian America* 90/91: 251–268.

Tuan, Mia. 1998. *Forever Foreigners or Honorary Whites: The Asian Ethnic Experience Today.* New Brunswick, N.J.: Rutgers University Press.

U.S. Census. 2000. Available at http://www.census.gov (accessed 14 March 2006).

U.S. Immigration and Naturalization Service (USINS). 1997. *Statistical Yearbook of the Immigration and Naturalization Service.* Washington, D.C.: U.S. Government Printing Office.

van den Berghe, Pierre. 1981. *The Ethnic Phenomenon.* New York: Elsevier.

———. 1990. *Human Family Systems.* Prospect Heights, Ill.: Waveland.

Vecoli, Rudolph J. 1977. Cult and Occult in Italian-American Culture: The Persistence of Religious Heritage. Pp 25–47 in Randall M. Miller and Thomas D. Marzik (eds.), *Immigrants and Religion in Urban America.* Philadelphia: Temple University Press.

Wallace, Anthony F. C. 1966. *Religion: An Anthropological View.* New York: Random House.

Warner, Lloyd, and Leo Srole. 1945. *The Social Systems of American Ethnic Groups.* New Haven: Yale University Press.

Warner, Stephen R. 1993. Work in Progress towards a New Paradigm for the Sociological Study of Religion in the United States. *American Journal of Sociology* 98: 1044–1093.

Warner, Stephen R., and Judith G. Wittner. 1998. *Gatherings in Diaspora.* Philadelphia: Temple University Press.

Williams, Raymond Brady. 1988. *Religions of Immigrants from India and Pakistan.* New York: Cambridge University Press.

Woo, Deborah. 2000. *Glass Ceiling and Asian Americans: The New Face of Workplace Barriers.* Walnut Creek, Calif.: AltaMira Press.

Yancey, William, Richard Juliani, and Eugene Erikson. 1976. Emergent Ethnicity: A Review and Reformulation. *American Sociological Review* 41: 391–403.

Yang, Fenggang. 1999. *Chinese Christians in America: Conversion, Assimilation, and Adhesive Identities.* University Park: Pennsylvania State University Press.

Yoon, Paul Jong-Chul. 2005. Christian Identity, Ethnic Identity: Music Making and Prayer Practices among 1.5- and Second-Generation Korean-American Christians. Ph.D. dissertation, Columbia University, New York.

Yu, Eui-Young, and Peter Choe. 2003. 100 Years of American History: The Korean American Population. Powerpoint presentation given at the First

National Convention, Waikiki, Hawaii, January 10–13. (Powerpoint slide 16.) Available at http://www.calstatela.edu/centers/ckaks/ (accessed May 19, 2006).

Yuh, Ji-Yeon. 2004. *Beyond the Shadow of Camptown: Korean Military Brides in America.* New York: New York University Press.

Zhou, Min. 2004. Are Asian Americans Becoming White? *Context* 3 (1): 29–37.

Zhou, Min, and James V. Gatewood. 2000. *Contemporary Asian America: A Multidisciplinary Reader.* New York: New York University Press.

Zhou, Min, Carl L. Bankston III, and Rebecca Kim. 2002. Rebuilding Spiritual Lives in the New Land: Religious Practices among Southeast Asian Refugees in the United States. Pp. 37–70 in Pyong Gap Min and Jung Ha Kim (eds.), *Religions in Asian America: Building Faith Communities.* Walnut Creek, Calif.: AltaMira Press.

Index

About the Author

Rebecca Y. Kim is Assistant Professor of Sociology at Pepperdine University. She received her Ph.D. at the University of California, Los Angeles, in 2003. She has published in numerous journals and books, including *Sociology of Religion, Sociological Quarterly, International Migration Review, Religions in Asian America, Asian American Religion,* and *Asian American Youth Culture.* She is currently working on a project on multiethnic congregations and enjoys spending time with her family and new baby, Christyn.